Clear and comforting help for those who suffer guilt feelings because they did not receive the miracle they prayed for . . . it can help turn the questions of "why did this happen to me?" What can this mean?"
—Christian Review

When There Is No MIRACLE

Robert L. Wise

Regal Books

A Division of GL Publications
Ventura, California, U.S.A.

Other good reading:
Yet Will I Trust Him by Peg Rankin
Glorify God and Enjoy Him Forever by Peg Rankin

Published by Regal Books
A Division of GL Publications
Ventura, California 93006
Printed in U.S.A.

Library of Congress Catalog Card No. 77-089394

ISBN 0-8307-0582-1

8 9 10 11 12 13 14 15 / 91 90 89

Rights for publishing this book in other languages are contracted by Gospel
Literature International (GLINT) foundation. GLINT also provides technical
help for the adaptation, translation, and publishing of Bible study resources
and books in scores of languages worldwide. For further information, contact
GLINT, Post Office Box 488, Rosemead, California, 91770, U.S.A., or the
publisher.

contents

Foreword   **9**

Preface   **11**

Introduction   **15**

one   Why Doesn't God Do Something?   **21**

two   God Speaks Through Silence   **37**

three   The Paradox of Pain   **57**

four   The Profit from Pain   **73**

five   The Power in Pain   **95**

six   Who's to Blame?   **113**

seven   The Inevitable Hour   **135**

eight   While Waiting for a Miracle   **149**

nine   When I Lay Me Down to Sleep   **163**

foreword

Reading Dr. Robert Wise's manuscript at this particular time in my life has meant fresh quietness and assurance, for on this very day I enter a California hospital for surgery. During the past three or four years I have participated in many healing services, read many books on the subject, and yet "There was no miracle." The thorough way in which Robert Wise has anticipated the questions facing a person (with no miracle) has touched me deeply because in every chapter there is fresh strength to see God's long-range viewpoint instead of my short-sighted one.

My spirit has been healed, my heart cleansed and fortified over and over again, by such words as, "Every experience God gives me, every person He puts in my life, is the perfect preparation for the future that only He can see .... He is at work bringing order to confusion and strength to sickness."

We can exchange our tired old question: "Why did this happen to me?" for "What can this mean? How will God use this?"

Rosalind Rinker, July, 1977

preface

And so the pendulum swings.

In each age and decade the emphases, the sounds, and the concerns make a shift. As people move forward in history, their needs and insights travel with them. And so the pendulum has swung in matters of faith again.

Fifteen years ago no one took the question of miracles very seriously. They were rumored to have happened, but not in anyone's memory. The church held them as part of the venerated relics of the past—the apostolic era had come and gone and so had miracles.

Ten years ago the whispers began. Stories drifted in about extraordinary goings-on way out on the fringes: the miraculous had come again! But no one in the respectable uptown mainline denominations had time for

11

such excesses. The liberals laughed at such nonsense; the evangelicals wondered about the reports; the conservatives thought at least they ought to go and see. But miracles certainly were not in style. Yet the pendulum had indeed begun to swing.

So, in this decade God's surprise has come pell-mell. Amazement upon amazement has confronted ecclesiastical leaders and the average churchmen. As the modern charismatic movement spread across every denomination and swept through every communion, a new day was born. A fresh teaching engulfed the church like wildfire: *you can look for and expect a miracle!* A daily adventure with God into the incredible and unexpected is open to you!

Make no mistakes, I applaud the prairie fire. My life and ministry have been caught up in the new work of the Holy Spirit. What an exciting decade in which to minister! While the new fire has reduced some ministers to cinders, most who came in honest openness find living waters beyond their dreams. Dying denominations are being revived, and institutionalized churches are receiving divine shock waves that revive their encrusted hearts. But, most important, individuals with hurts and needs find that God does make a difference. At this very moment the Holy Spirit's power is more available than ever.

Yet, in the midst of honest enthusiasm and genuine appreciation for God's grace, many teachers have gone too far. New teachings are arising that are not what Jesus taught nor what the Scriptures promise. The pendulum has swung too far.

These teachers say that any failure to receive a miracle is the result of sin or unbelief. You ought to be able to command God to work on your behalf. If He doesn't come through, then something is wrong with you!

One of my major reasons for writing this book is to confront these teachings, clear up the confusion and bring reassurance to thousands of sincere people who are walking by faith through days of turmoil and trauma. You *ought* to believe and anticipate the extraordinary intervening power of God, but God does not move at the snap of anyone's fingers, nor by the quoting of Scripture verses out of context. It is possible that you are missing the greatest miracle: that His sovereign hand is moving through every single event of your life whether the moment is exalted and exhilarating or tempestuous and traumatic.

Another reason for this book is to help you understand the problem of suffering. Sooner or later—Christian or pagan—we will all have to face tragedy in very personal terms. What then shall we say? How shall we explain the haunting whys and wherefores?

I quite readily recognize that this book is not a definitive statement on pain and suffering. Frankly, I doubt if a complete answer will ever be written. Rather, I offer practical suggestions for those of you who struggle with the issues as they unfold in your own living rooms.

The following is not a theologian's meditation but the product of a pastor's daily rounds of hospitals, homes and haunts of affliction. From my journeys, I have learned that we need to gain a correct perspective *before* we come to a crisis. Once we descend into the swirl of emotion and confusion, the dilemmas loom so large that we find it difficult to see beyond the question marks. I hope these insights will more adequately prepare you to recognize God's presence when turmoil raises a dust that will not allow you to open your eyes.

Moreover, should the days run ahead of the answers, my prayers preface the writing of every page. I have sought God's help in finding clarity to lift the answer up high enough to overpower the questions. I write for people who hurt.

One other word of explanation must be added. I introduce each chapter through a fictional device called "A Personal Conversation with Jesus." In these imaginary conversations I capsulize the tone and perception of each chapter. The conversation is meant to intrigue and challenge you. That and nothing more. Christians commonly say to one another, "the Lord told me," or, "the Lord has shown me." In that vein, these conversations are an artistic expression of what I believe the Lord has told *me* as I have walked my own path. I claim nothing more.

Finally, I must express my gratitude to those who have labored with me to make this manuscript possible. As always the encouragement of my dear sister in the faith, Maria Ann Hirschman (Hansi), has been invaluable in motivating my writing. In addition I can never thank Jane Carter Cole White enough for her time in teaching me something of the finer details of the art of writing. And every writer ought to have a Fritz Ridenour for his editor. His understanding and promptings put these pages together. My sister-in-law, Rose Ann Howlett, ran a thousand errands helping me get the book together and I thank her. But none of my books would ever have been written without the faithful, persistent work of my secretary, Dorothy Waltz. Her endless hours at the typewriter made the manuscript a reality. Though not miracles, our friends are one of God's richest interventions in our lives!

Robert L. Wise
May 1, 1977
Oklahoma City, Oklahoma

introduction

Across the room from where I am writing, my son is lying in a hospital bed with his leg in traction. Fortunately the lacerations on his face are not deep and shouldn't leave any real scars. The deep gash on his chest is another matter. As the steering wheel bent and shattered to pieces, the jagged steering column caught him in the ribs like a Roman lance.

He hasn't required too many pain pills. His dislocated hip seems to have slipped back into place sufficiently so that if the bone fragments move equally well, he won't have to have surgery.

The boy sitting beside him in the front seat didn't fare as well. He is in surgery having his jaw wired. As he went through the windshield, his jaw was broken in two places, his tongue badly cut and his face lacerated.

The boys in the back seat weren't as badly injured: one broke his thumb; one lost two teeth; the other only received lacerations and a black eye.

The irony of it all is that this pain has come from absolutely nothing they did, deserved, or for which they were responsible. They are all high school wrestlers and good boys. Todd just happened to be driving down the street when another driver recklessly pulled into his lane of traffic and hit the carload of teenagers head-on. The man was completely on the wrong side of the street.

In just a few weeks wrestling season will begin. These boys won't be there. Will they ever wrestle again? It's too early to know, but obviously it is a painful question that compounds the injury.

Now why should this happen? Why should these boys have such a blow? Why did they have to be on that street at that precise moment this man pulled over?

Why? Why my son? Why my car? Why my friends?

This hospital room is more than an appropriate place for me to meet my old enemy "Mr. Why" again. We first got acquainted in this very building. In fact, it was on this exact floor and in this exact corridor I bumped into him about 10 years ago. Just two rooms down the hall, one of my friends and most faithful parishioners was dying of a brain tumor. As I watched Gene deteriorate and the bulge on his head grow, I discovered how haunting Mr. Why can be with his inopportune visits.

Yes, I thought about death and tragedy in college. I majored in humanities and rather enjoyed reading the great tragic novels of history. Those intriguing plots and sad characters conveyed great feelings that were so compelling. (They always are, when off in the distance.)

And seminary hadn't ignored the problem. We discussed suffering and had stimulating rap sessions about ol' Job and his boils. Our expertise in responding intellectually to the problem was remarkable. (In retrospect it *was* remarkable because we knew nothing about what we were so brilliantly expounding.)

But in room 1037 it all became a painfully different experience. Gene was vigorous. He was bright with an excellent career. He had two boys to raise. Moreover, he was an exceptional Christian. So why should he be dying? Particularly why should he be dying this slow painful death that by inches robbed him of sight, touch, feeling, and hope?

Why? Why? Why?

Yes, the suffering of the innocent is fascinating in a debating hall. It is nauseating and debilitating in the hospital room.

Mr. Why left me exposed. He revealed the nakedness of my thinking. Emotionally he made me feel like a fool. My counsel to the needy in the halls of tragedy was pale, anemic and hollow. Inside me something deep and fundamental cried out for revenge. I decided I would never again let his passing go unchallenged. I would find the tools for counterattack!

As I sit here in the room with Todd I remember still another time Mr. Why and I met in this very hospital. It was just two stories downstairs that Tate struggled with a tumor that ate away in his shattered leg.

Tate was our "little boy." Always quiet, he is like his mother. They are both blond, blue-eyed Creek Indians. They carry the Indian trait of a quietness that, like deep water, is filled with perceptiveness. Their gentleness is born of sensitivity.

One fall afternoon I got a call from the school. When I arrived I found Tate curled up on the school couch in deep pain. He kept biting into his hand to fight back the tears. My gosh, he was tough for a six-year-old! He had shattered his thighbone while playing football. I carried him into the station wagon and on to the hospital. I then left the hospital. Of all things, I was just minutes away from conducting a funeral service.

I expected that his leg would be set in a cast and, no doubt, after a brief stay in the hospital, he would go home. But it wasn't that simple. When I returned to the hospital I found his mother white and taut—her eyes carried a different message.

There was a hidden tumor growing in Tate's leg. The bone broke because of the weakness created by the growth. Moreover, the tumor was eating at the point of the growth line in the bone. If the trauma of the break started to spread, his leg would be permanently stunted. He would always have one thigh bone the length of his six-year-old leg.

I felt the deep gnawing of fear and apprehension spread through every fiber of my body.

That afternoon stretched into eight torturous weeks in traction. It went on and on with a debilitating body cast that Tate had to wear into the hot, sweaty summer.

We began to notice the strange way people looked at our child, painfully bent forward in a position that never let him completely relax. Being with him day and night we hadn't noticed that he was growing thinner and paler. Finally someone asked about the tumor.

Would it spread? Could it be fatal? After all, he was looking worse and worse. He just didn't seem to improve.

I walked to a nearby lake one afternoon and for the first time realized that what seemed like an ordinary childhood accident might become the end of this small winsome little life. The nights of sleeping on the hospital floor, the months of disordered family life, the professional detachment in dealing with other people's pain all fell apart.

I started sobbing uncontrollably. I had prayed. I did believe. What wrong had we done to deserve this? Why attack this little boy who was so small and fragile? Why us? In many ways we had sacrificed for the things of God, and now this. Why? I wanted to scream and curse everything in the universe.

Gratefully, I can report that Tate did recover. The long summer stretched into the fall. Bone graft surgery succeeded. By the time snow fell, he was on his feet again. Today he is as active as ever. Yet those tortuous months left a permanent mark on us all. We know that no one is exempt from pain.

And now, because of a careless driver's twist of the steering wheel, Mr. Why had come to pay another call. As I gazed on Todd's broken body I faced him again. He leered at me from behind everything I believed. My wrestling with him was not over. A new round of questions was forced on me and I was determined to find better answers.

In a sterile, impersonal, hospital room this book was born. Countless hours have been spent in those hard hospital chairs; they never became comfortable. I thank the friends I met there for sharing their stories. Those imposing dilemmas helped shape these pages. Many of my acquaintances have suffered far greater tragedies than I and have known deeper crushing pain. Nevertheless, it is no longer an eager seminarian interested in difficult questions who picks up the pen. I am now a hesitant veteran who knows how strange and twisting life's roads can be.

I remember the sage wisdom of one of my college professors. After years of study in religion and philosophy he came to his own conclusion. He felt no one could really write anything that would cover all tragedy with a full satisfying answer. "Rather," he remarked, "each of us takes the best answer he can find and just lives with it. As the years pass what can't really be explained has a way of wearing down into one's total life pattern. If we are blessed, we find a grace that will assure us that what couldn't ever be really explained was in the end redemptive."

To help you see the truth of these words is the ultimate purpose of this book. I know that if you look deeply and long enough you will find grace was always holding your life together. What couldn't be fathomed, could still be redemptive.

one

———————A Personal Conversation with Jesus———————

My mind was so filled with wonder that I thought His teaching itself was intoxicating. To listen to His words was to soar to high cliffs of insight that left the whole world far below.

"Oh, Jesus, what mysteries you unravel. I want to understand everything. Tell me all of the secrets of the Father's will."

Always He was kind but firm. "No, you have not been given to know the breadth of every plan. The riddles of the unseen are crucial to your journey."

"But Master, the road bends and I'm not sure of the direction. There are forks in the path and no marker to point the better way. I am left with so much uncertainty."

Jesus bent down and picked up a handful of pebbles from the dusty trail. He bounced them in His palm and then flung them over the terrain. "Do they seem to fly in a pointless flight? And yet they all do come home again to their mother, the earth. Doesn't My Father esteem you infinitely more?"

"Oh, of course, Master. Always."

"Then enjoy the mystery of the road. All that counts is that at the end of the journey you will find Him there."

Why Doesn't God Do SOMETHING?

"But wasn't there something more you could have done?"

"Let me assure you, we did everything that was medically possible. The best possible care is right here in this hospital."

"But couldn't there have been something more? He was so strong and so healthy. It just can't be."

Her tone was more like the pleading of a prayer. She wasn't really looking for the doctor's assurance. She knew this was the best hospital they could find. That's why they took that wild midnight ambulance ride.

"Surely there could have been another treatment or operation or medicine or something. He was so young and I was so proud of that boy."

It was there that her voice began to trail off into a distant soliloquy that came up from her soul. Only something deep within herself could really answer back. She knew there were no more remedies to be tried or prayers to be said. Still something maternal wanted to clutch at the air and pray until it would become solid, and the ugly reality in that unfeeling hospital corridor would be changed. But it wouldn't. It wouldn't ever again.

They prayed for a miracle. They believed for a miracle. Moreover, they desperately hoped for a miracle. But now it wouldn't ever come. Nothing more could be done.

When her son slammed into the other motorcycle his body became a flying projectile. Without a protective helmet nothing stood between him and the unyielding, unforgiving concrete. At a speed of 50 miles an hour, flesh had little hope against rock. In those split seconds, pain and haunting questions were forever indelibly etched in the soul of that family.

"We did believe a miracle would happen. Wasn't there something more that *could* have been done?"

The Faces of Your Tragedies

Every time we think about tragedy, suffering, disaster, and death, the questions come with a face attached. There is someone out there who had deep, personal significance for us. Tragedy always brings these faces back to us. We remember how real and final calamity can be.

If the face is distant or comes from secondhand experience, the whole matter isn't so pressing and can be more leisurely considered. It is much easier to think about these things when they can be held at arm's length.

23

But life allows no such leisure. Sooner or later tragedy will march into your own living room. It is only a matter of time until your emotions will be assaulted and your composure ripped by the sound of a siren in the night. You can't ever choose the time or place for pain to strike.

So, I write these descriptions with the tenderest intent. I know how excruciating and annihilating it is when that face of your personal tragedy appears. You are sure that no one in all the world has ever felt such a pain.

Perhaps you find yourself saying, "Wasn't there something more that could have been done?"

You may find these memories bring deep animosity. Not hurt as much as hostility fills your thoughts. Perhaps, if you admit it, you desire revenge on God! When we look our doubts full in the face we want to know, "Why didn't God do something more?"

"Why wasn't there a miracle? Couldn't there have been an intervention? Others say it happened to them. Some make eloquent speeches about how God made the difference. Well, why didn't that happen for that cherished face of my memories?"

I'm not only thinking of the pain of death or physical agony. Tragedy is manifold. Perhaps the living tragedies that go on and on are even more difficult to accept and understand.

What about the child who doesn't die but is permanently disabled and virtually reduced to a vegetable? Remember the illness that passes but leaves someone forever disfigured? Or what about the marriage "made in heaven" that ends, dividing children between parents? Was God not interested in doing something with such defeats?

The face in your memory may be that of a business

partner. You prayed together about this new venture. True, you were going to make some money, but it was clear that God was to be a partner in it. His blessing would mean you could really give more than generously to His causes. Yes sir, this was going to be God's business!

Then the tide turned. The market went down while inflation went up. You tried everything.

"Pray?"

"Are you kidding? We never in our lives prayed harder."

But the inevitable came. When you went bankrupt it wasn't just an embarrassment. The failure wasn't just a hardship on your families. It was more like God was either unable or unwilling to do anything!

The faces in our memories may take many forms and come from many directions. But they still amount to the same thing. God was silent. On behalf of those whom we cherish through loving memory, we want to know something deeper.

Christians talk a great deal about what God does. Do they have much to say about the apparent vacuums created when He doesn't act?

I also know about that "apparent vacuum." For years my mother has been lying helpless in a nursing home. She requires constant care since she is no longer able to feed herself. A horrible, crippling arteriosclerosis began robbing her mind about eight years ago. She was always so intelligent, so skilled at math. Tucked away in her was a secret pride in being a good "businesswoman." Then she began to have difficulty expressing herself. We began to notice she couldn't find things. On and on the condition developed until she was unable to recognize even her family.

Frankly, I don't go to see her very often. I avoid visits

because I just can't stand it. To walk into her room and find nothing behind her eyes is unbearable for me. I shuffle things around, make light conversation, act very professional, and leave quickly because I don't know how to face my emotions.

She was a terrific mother who struggled to make life special for me and my sister. What did she deserve? A happy, rich, old age in which she could enjoy her grandchildren would be only just. Nothing in her life called for such a final defeat.

For her there has been no miracle. Her face is always before me as I ponder suffering.

Wait, I Do Believe in Miracles!

Before we go any further, let's get one thing clear. I *do* believe in miracles. In spite of everything I've seen in the "vacuum," I *do* believe in God's intervening presence. Unless you understand and believe that I do know that God breaks in and changes things, you won't be able to share my discoveries of faith.

It is true that much of contemporary Christianity doesn't believe in the miraculous. Liberal protestantism tends not to believe God is at work in special and unusual ways. Many of these scholars and preachers don't believe that Jesus really performed miracles at all.

A hundred different writers have explained away the miracle stories of Jesus' ministry. Some have spiritualized the miracles so they carry only symbolic meaning. Others have noted they come from a prescientific era. They interpret the stories as being good public relations for the early church. They tell us to forget such unusual happenings. "Learn to live life on a 'tough' basis," they admonish. These preachers are sure Jesus only meant to give us authenticity in the face of adversity.

Someone is always popping up to explain away Old

26

Testament miracles. But what all these explanations boil down to is a basic disbelief that the unusual happened at all.

These rationalizations are much like the story of the child coming home from Sunday School to tell his father about Moses at the Red Sea. The six-year-old described the Israelites putting down pontoon bridges for their jeeps to cross on. Then as Pharaoh approached and his army came over the bridges, they were dynamited and the whole Egyptian army sank in one fell swoop!

The father calmly asked his enthusiastic son if that was really the way it happened. The child's response was, "No, but if I told you what they really said at church, you sure wouldn't believe it!"

The skeptics' versions of Christianity have become empty ethical shells with a dead center. The power has gone out. The result? When people of this persuasion try to explain death, tragedy, and difficulty, they only tend to reinforce our doubts!

I want you to know I totally disagree with these schools of thought. I very, very much *do* believe in miracles!

Oral Roberts made "Expect a miracle!" into a national slogan. I agree with him. That's where I live! I do expect miracles. Even more, I want you to look for God's dramatic interventions. I don't want tragedy to blur your vision and make you miss the overwhelming ways in which God is surprising us all the time. I don't believe I could face the emotionally staggering situations in life if I didn't know that God is constantly at hand, working His will and way.

What Is a Miracle?

We need a working definition of miracle: *A miracle is an event that conflicts with the laws of nature and is*

27

therefore caused by a supernatural agency. There are probably more technical definitions but this covers what most people generally mean by a "miracle."

But the biblical conception of the miraculous has much more punch. The emphasis is on the Greek word, *dunamis* or "power": *Miracles are the natural consequences of the power of God.* Consider:

> In Jewish literature 'the Power' was used as a name for God ... Disbelief in the miracles is usually the result of disbelief in the biblical conception of God as the source of all power or in Christ as the veritable incarnation of the dunamis of God (cf. 1 Cor. 1:24: "Christ the dunamis of God"[1]). The God of the Bible is he of whom alone it may with propriety be said: panta dunata, "all things are possible."[2]

Because God is all-powerful, extraordinary events are sure to follow!

Actually, Saint Augustine would take exception with our first definition of a miracle. He cautioned that miracles are not really in conflict with the laws of nature. They are only in conflict with what we currently know about natural law. He taught that God does not perform irrational acts. But our limited perception of the universe keeps us from understanding how His every move fits together with what we can understand. Augustine's qualification is very important as we shall see in chapter 3.

We should further realize that the *dunamis* of God was passed through Jesus Christ to His church. The New Testament gives overwhelming evidence that miracles were a common occurrence in the everyday life of Christians.[3] I find nothing in the Bible to cause me to conclude that miracle power ever left the church.

So here's my personal definition: *A miracle is a demonstration of God's power breaking into our lives at a point of need in such a dramatic way that the situation is immediately changed.* Not only do I believe this is possible, I have experienced the result. Here are two examples.

Why I Believe in Miracles

Remember my six-year-old son Tate who had the shattered, tumorous leg? He would not even have made it to age six without God's gracious intervention.

Shortly after his birth, we began to be aware of an unusual skin color. Since he had Indian background, we assumed he was going to be an unusually dark "red-skinned" child. But the skin color was strange. Gradually the shading took on a more yellowish cast.

One morning as the sunlight streamed in striking his small, innocent face, we discovered his eyes were turning yellow. He was jaundiced! Being so close we hadn't caught the subtlety of change. He was turning yellow by degrees.

Immediately the tiny bundle was rushed for medical examination. The grave response of the doctor spoke volumes. He quietly called the hospital and we went straight to the surgical floor.

A congenital liver defect was forcing bile into his system. The facts were simple. At six weeks of age and under six pounds in weight, surgery was a complete hazard. It would be like operating on a rabbit. The chances were nil. But that wasn't the worst news. To the doctor's knowledge, no one had ever survived this condition. Generally an infant wasted away.

I was too shocked even to worry about the "why" questions. I found myself walking dazed through a maze of unknown emotions. I was too young and out of touch with my feelings even to know how to respond.

My wife and I were young Christians and not sure how to proceed. Somewhere we had heard we were to trust and pray. We did.

That evening I insisted my wife go home. I would spend the night with this baby. I felt I could "take it" better. Little did I know!

As the night wore on I went through the funeral and the burial a hundred times. Intermittently I prayed. By morning I was a basket case.

Barbara arrived very early. Unlike me, she was quite calm and composed. Her simple faith had given her an entirely different experience through the dark hours. After praying she had sensed a great calm and assurance that allowed her to fall asleep. In that peaceful sleep a clear dream took shape. She could vividly remember dreaming that the surgery completely corrected the condition. In detail she described what would happen and how a by-pass would be constructed. Confidently she shared that he would live and would be a special child.

It was all too much for me. I couldn't get what she was saying. My vision had been an open grave with the family standing beside a small casket. When they came with the long, black surgical cart, I was overwhelmed.

Three hours later, the doctor burst into the room. He was elated! He couldn't believe it! Obviously the surgical success was a first for him. He was amazed with the result. As he carefully shared his discovery of how they had constructed a by-pass for the bile duct, it was like watching a movie. I had heard the exact description three hours before.

God did a special thing in our lives. That little boy was living proof of His miraculous power!

Do I believe in miracles? You bet!

Let me share further. Several years ago I became convinced that the church ought to pray for the sick, believing that God could immediately intervene. It was no small leap of faith for me to share my convictions with the congregation, asking them to gather to pray. I wasn't sure whether God would honor my convictions or the church would run me off.

The results were an exciting new chapter in my ministry. Once a month a special evening service of "The Healing Christ" was held. The sick came forward to kneel and accept grace. Over a period of months I saw amazing results.

The night June came to pray is the most vivid in my mind. Her ankles were deteriorating and nothing seemed to help. Already she was in corrective shoes and faced a wheelchair in the not too distant future. The radiant Christian woman was suffering with nagging pain that nothing seemed to help.

She knelt in prayer for someone else. How like her that was! But I moved by her side and felt prompted to pray for her ankles. Together we claimed God's promises and I felt an unusual confidence that something special was happening in those moments of prayer.

A week later her phone call came. "Robert, I didn't want to say anything until I went to the doctor. But when I walked away from that altar I knew I was healed. My feet hadn't felt that way in years."

I was astonished. Though her conversation continued in a quite factual manner, I was awestruck.

"Today, I went back for X-rays. The doctor was flabbergasted. The deposits of calcium were gone. Everything in my bones was straight and correct. Praise the Lord!"

Praise the Lord indeed.

I think you have my point. I unquestionably believe God breaks into our lives in dramatic moments that immediately change the situation at hand.

But Don't Play Charades

Perhaps you feel the same way I do. No one has to prove miracles to you. You believe! If so, you may even be all the more vulnerable to the problem: What happens to a believer and his faith when nothing happens? How do you really deal with life when the miracle doesn't seem to appear?

When we are convinced of God's power and our world falls apart, our problems may be even more frustrating to live with. The disaster may now become compounded by guilt, despair, or even irrationality.

One of the saddest side results of this dilemma are the people who have to slide into a fantasy world. They still hold on to what they desperately want to believe is true while living with what they cannot escape or face.

A young nurse shared a conversation she had with a patient. The lady was wheelchair-bound and appeared to be permanently immobilized. The nurse inquired about the lady's health and state of mind.

"Oh, I've had a miracle. I have already been healed."

The concerned nurse's face registered consternation. Obviously the lady was unable to move her body.

Realizing the obvious contradiction, the invalid stated with absolute conviction. "*I* have had a miracle, but my legs just don't believe it yet."

That might sound like a cruel joke if it were not so tragic. Behind her confident assertions lurked sheer terror. There was no faith explanation that was acceptable to this woman for her immobility. Somewhere she had developed the idea that if she said she was healed often enough, she would be! This was her definition of faith.

But to her the prospect of the absence of a miracle meant the loss of God. She had no other way to explain the dilemma. Behind her confident smile and definite statements was complete desperation.

When we have no good explanation for the lack of a miracle, all varieties of self-deception sneak in. The result is a game of charades that calls itself faith. We can play at it for a time. But sooner or later our pretense must end.

Religious charades result when we clothe our fears in the dress of faith. Intuitively, we sense that it is easier to disguise what we dread than it is to expose it. But by this disguise we make religious promises our allies in the inner struggle to ignore our anxieties. So when we don't receive a miracle we may try even more frantically to insist on what we don't want to face.

Simplistic sermons and platitudes that lift scriptural promises out of context only encourage our problem. They dismiss unavoidable realities of life with a burst of enthusiastic belief.

How often has the following passage been thrown in for good measure? "All things are possible to him who believes" (Mark 9:23). Indeed, this is one of the greatest and most comforting passages in the entire Bible. Out of my own life, I can testify that the promise is true.

But if I apply this promise from God in an attempt to retreat from reality, I turn this promise into a lie. The words become a text through which *my hopes* get mistaken for *God's* actual *intentions.*

I can't forget the experience of Chuck, a teenage boy who died of cancer. Near the end of his time of suffering he decided to write to a "faith healer," a man who was known locally. This faith healer preached that he would pray and give careful personal attention to any who called on his ministry for help.

As a final act of frustration, Chuck poured out his deepest inner feelings of apprehension. He wrote a detailed description of his fears. The preacher promised absolute wholeness; all you need is "faith" if you want to be healed. Chuck's plea was that the healer would help him realize the victory in his illness. He was desperate. He needed to know what was wrong. What more could he do to make his faith work?

A few weeks later, the dying boy received a form letter. With the usual clichéd, hackneyed phrases, aimed at getting the gullible to send more money, the sterile page promised that they were "praying for him."

The letter did not acknowledge receiving Chuck's personal letter with the probing questions. No one even had the decency or concern to recognize a passionate plea for understanding; no one responded to the loneliness a youngster was feeling in facing death. All the organization offered were simplistic promises, lifted out of their biblical contexts. And a request for money.

My young friend was shattered. As he was going down for the third time the healer threw him a lead weight.

Truly, the pauses of God demand better explanations than this. If anyone had cared he could have led Chuck down a positive path to death. By squarely facing his questions, someone could have helped Chuck settle any guilt or doubt he had about himself and the adequacy of his faith. In the end both of them could have shared the real victory Jesus gives us over death.

To tell Chuck that "all things are possible to him who believes," without sharing with him the many possibilities open to him other than physical healing, reduces our great God to our small human formulas. God does not respond just because we believe we have fulfilled all the requirements. He does not jump when we pull the right levers. He was here before we came and will still be here long after we are dust. Mystery must forever surround many of the Father's intentions.

I cannot be dishonest. Don't count on me to help play charades! God's promises offer more than they seem to at face value. I am deeply concerned that we gain insight into the meaning of these times of seeming hesitations on God's part. Our life journey may have its riddles, but in the beginning, along the way, and at the end, God is still here.

Some Concluding Thoughts

Inevitably, we are confronted by life's frighteningly painful moments. We pray, believe and are willing to do anything to change these unwanted circumstances. With deep fervor we ask God for a miracle.

And across the span of our lives, we will see Him move in many clear ways. We know God has intervened. But other hours will come when the same faith brings no visible results. Out of these valleys of despair we ask, "Why was there no miracle?"

Human experience and Christian maturity demand we go deeper into the unseen ways of God. To cover the absence of the miracle we asked for with simplistic explanations, "you didn't believe" or "you didn't have faith," is to invite disaster. Any answer that avoids reality only sets us up to be deceived. Therefore, we must push on and ask the difficult questions our doubts raise.

My personal experiences have not led me to understand every mystery in God's hidden strategy. But I have learned a very important truth: the empty times can bring a profound depth of insight and understanding that can be found nowhere else.

These riddles in our daily experience are critical to our personal development. And, in the end, they help us

35

to walk in total confidence, not only by what we can see but also by what we believe.

Some Questions to Ponder

1. Have you ever asked, "Why didn't God do something more?" What was God's answer when Paul raised a similar question? (See 2 Cor. 12:8-10.)

2. This chapter gives three definitions of a "miracle." Which one do you feel most comfortable with? Can the first definition always be applied to healing?

3. In light of the author's own definition of miracle, did Paul receive a miracle (2 Cor. 12:10)? Was it what he asked for?

4. Is faith a way of knowing where you are going all of the time? Or is faith just trusting that God is leading?

5. Some of the following verses have been "lifted from their contexts" and therefore give another meaning. Read each passage in its entirety and tell what you think it means:
   a. "I will restore you to health and I will heal you of your wounds" (Jer. 30:17).
   b. "By His scourging we are healed" (Isa. 53:5).
   c. "I can do all things through Him who strengthens me" (Phil. 4:13).
   d. "And we know that God causes all things to work together for good" (Rom. 8:28).

Notes

1. See also Acts; 1 Corinthians 5:4; 12:28-31; Ephesians 3:16.
2. Alan Richardson, *A Theological Word Book of the Bible* (New York: Macmillan Publishing Company, Inc., 1950), p. 152.
3. Dr. Eric L. Titus, *Christian Word Book* (Nashville: Graded Press, 1968), p. 194.

two

_____A Personal Conversation with Jesus_____

When I first encountered Him, His sense of destiny drew me even closer. Never had I seen anyone who had such certainty and surety with His every action. This was a man who knew where He was going! The longer I listened the more that verdict was confirmed.

So one night at supper I asked Him about my own unanswered question. "Jesus, you have made sense out of my aimless life. Yet, so much of what I have experienced seems to have no purpose whatsoever. Why can't I understand the final reasons for all that I have suffered?"

He picked up the loaf from the table and ripped the bread apart. Holding the torn halves He stared into my eyes.

"My Father does not let us see life from beginning to end. But we know that His loving hands hold even the pieces that are torn."

My doubts insisted on one more word. "But how do I know that His love holds the broken portions?"

He laid down the loaves and reached for my hand. His touch was warm and firm. The answer was simple. "You know me, don't you?"

God
Speaks
Through
SILENCE

George was 19 when the first lump appeared. Until that moment he was a carefree, handsome young athlete with a college scholarship before him. But the doctor's diagnosis of cancer started George on the slow and inevitable rearrangement of every plan and dream.

The tragedy was not his alone. As the disease spread through his body, so deterioration permeated his whole family. As George's muscular body shrank, his parents' marriage dried up because they could not come to grips with the tragedy.

Wanda, his mother, was a 40-year-old woman whose life had been almost totally invested in her son. When the first cancer reports came in, Wanda proclaimed she had absolute faith in God's power. Her son was too important to her to have anything but a complete recovery. Yet, as his condition worsened, she vacillated between trust and terror.

As the pain consumed her son's body, Wanda became obsessed with why the tragedy had happened to *her*. Her inability to find solid footing set the stage for a total loss of perspective. When George died, her marriage ended and the last vestige of her faith dissolved.

You may have experienced the same pangs of terror that gripped Wanda's life. While on one hand you wanted to believe in a miracle, you weren't getting any answers to your prayers. Deep within, your confidence seemed to be replaced by confusion. You could not make any sense out of what was happening or where you were going.

When our prayers seem to bring nothing but silence from God, it is natural for us to be bewildered. And soon, our apprehensions turn into a sense of deep misgiving. On every side, our doubts nag and nibble away at our self-confidence. We once thought of ourselves as people of strong faith, but now we don't know whether to believe or not.

You may feel as though you are the only person in the world to ever feel this way. Perhaps you're not sure anyone has ever been through such terrible pain. And you may be sure that all of your doubts are simply a confirmation that God has truly abandoned you.

At these times we all need a lot of help to regain our composure. We must find someone to help us make sense out of our questions and the vacuum we seem to have entered. Without help, we draw hasty conclusions that will make our situation even worse.

For example, we may easily deduce that our faith was simply naive. Perhaps, God doesn't really intervene on behalf of troubled people. Or, we may conclude that

God is really indifferent. His silence certainly seems to equate with lack of concern.

So we truly want to know if God *does* work during these times when our prayers do not seem to be answered. We need to be reassured that we can get through the night. If God isn't going to intervene immediately in our problem, at least we want the confidence that He is still working.

First, let me reassure you that you are not alone in your feeling of isolation and despair. Millions of people have experienced the same doubts and misgivings that are bombarding you. Because you feel that you are alone and forgotten doesn't mean that anything is wrong with you or your faith.

Second, it is normal for your emotions to twist the facts of your experience into contorted disfigurements of the truth. Suffering makes it difficult for all of us to make sense out of a bad situation.

During the dark hours we develop inner reservations that confuse us. Disorder seems to pervade our life and we panic. We cannot see the light at the end of the tunnel through which we are walking. Therefore, we need to recover our sense of perspective, to find reassurance that order is going to return to our daily lives. Though we don't understand how, it is possible to develop a new conviction that there is a final purpose for what is happening to us.

This can be very hard to do while you are experiencing the rotten moments. But until you get stabilized you will not be able to recognize the answers that are already around you. You will not be able to recognize how these difficult times can still have a constructive effect on your life.

As the apostles and the church recalled the life and ministry of Christ they discovered that God *does* work when there are no visible signs of His presence. They discovered that God's delay does not mean that God is absent. Even when life is broken like bread torn in half, the Father still holds the pieces in His hands. And Jesus told us that He, Himself, would be known in the breaking of the bread! (See Luke 22:19; 1 Cor. 10-16.)

I want to share three principles that will help get your personal situation back in focus. You can restore a sense of inner stability that will help you discover that God does still work on your problems during those times when your plea seems to fall on deaf ears.

Find Your Emotional Balance

When I first met May she was cowering against a brick wall. I will never forget her terror-filled eyes. This most attractive woman had taken on the look of a haunted war orphan. She had lost her emotional balance.

Because of a series of strange and questionable court decisions, she lost her children through the clever legal maneuvers of her ex-husband. All direction and purpose went out of her life. Alone and abandoned, she came to our city and, providentially, wandered into the church one Sunday morning.

May could not talk without crying. Simple decisions were painfully difficult. She had abandoned all hope and had lost her emotional balance and was stumbling in a maze that went nowhere.

We cannot go forward if we are off balance. The hard blows of life certainly knock all of us off center; nothing can affect our sense of perspective as much as being pulled from one extreme to the other. When this happens we must start over by finding solid footing.

As the months passed, May became more and more involved in the life of our church. The caring of new friends brought a desperately needed warmth to her life.

41

A new experience of God who truly is there began to form. May was able to regain her emotional balance. While the court decision did not change, she found a new joy in living.

Because of his time with Jesus, Peter was able to discover key insights that helped him put his emotions back in balance when the rest of the world was falling apart. He learned to recognize that God was at work even if, for the moment, Peter could not hear Him speaking.

Remember the night Peter betrayed his Lord three times? He was convinced that Jesus' ministry was over and God had abandoned him to the emptiness of disillusionment. Yet, in retrospect, Peter discovered that what he thought was an empty night was in reality the time of God's supreme work, not only on his behalf but also on the behalf of all humanity.

So Peter found a solution that kept him solidly balanced. He distilled the principle into a phrase: "Blessed be the God and Father of our Lord Jesus Christ, who according to His great *mercy* has caused us to be born again to a living hope through the resurrection of Jesus Christ from the dead" (1 Pet. 1:3, italics added).

Peter knew that God is merciful! When tragedy strikes we tend to feel that God is angry and vindictive. We become emotionally convinced that He is after us and the ones we love. In contrast, Peter believed the mercy of God was the context for everything that happened in his life. His confidence that God would only deal mercifully with him kept him in a balanced frame of mind. And you can have the same balance if you keep this same conviction foremost in your mind: no matter what is happening to you, God is still the Father of mercy.

Did Peter have a right to say that? Was he being

realistic? Well, his conviction about a living hope was formed while he was staring every possible doubt in the face. I have seen the place in Rome where tradition says Peter wrote his last letters and spent his final days. You must enter the Mamertine Prison by descending stone stairs into a musty and moldy dungeon. The dampness of drainage still comes through the stone walls and sinks into your emotions. There are no windows and the only light flickers from a candle. Just beyond this place, according to tradition, Peter, not wanting to be equal with His Lord, died on a cross upside down.

Quite possibly he wrote these words of hope while sitting against that cold wall. One wonders how he could be positive and stay balanced in such a condition. The answer is, Peter knew, regardless of the circumstances, that God had spread a canopy of mercy over him.

Peter went even further. Though he could not see through stone walls, though it seemed God was silent, Peter knew God was doing something special with his confinement.

Peter believed good was ahead for him. "So be truly glad! There is wonderful joy ahead, even though the going is rough for a while down here. These trials are only to test your faith, to see whether or not it is strong and pure. It is being tested as fire tests gold and purifies it—and your faith is far more precious to God than mere gold; so if your faith remains strong after being tried in the test tube of fiery trials, it will bring you much praise and glory and honor on the day of his return" (1 Pet. 1:6,7, *TLB*). Those silent moments from God were producing a completely tried and proven faith in Peter.

Be truly glad? He's got to be kidding! With all the runaway emotions we have inside of us, being positive seems impossible! Yet here is another secret of perspective: When we believe that good is ahead, that belief

43

restores a correct balance between pessimism and optimism.

The negative person tends not to see possibilities, so he estimates God's presence on the basis of what he can or cannot see. Thus his perspective is determined purely by what he can immediately perceive. Therefore, when suffering falls on him, his emotions become blinders.

Never let the present situation keep you from knowing that there is wonderful joy ahead. Aim for the glad heart. Certainly you can't be nonchalant about the bad things that happen to you, but believing that God's mercy is still surrounding your life will lift your eyes beyond the shadows around you; good is just over the horizon.

Right now, suspend judgment on what is happening to you and why it is happening. Wait and see. You may be surprised at the end of the story. Put your confidence in the simple truth that wonderful joy is ahead. Aim at the glad heart that will keep you balanced. This will hold promise and pain together in a creative tension.

Don't Be a Navel Gazer

To help you see through the silent times when there seems to be no miracle you should avoid habitual introspection. Chronic self-inspection will keep you from discovering that God is still at work.

When we become hopelessly mired down in endless introspection and self-preoccupation, we become so involved with the big "I" that our vision is obscured by our nose!

Ever hear about the modern day Job? Everything bad that could happen had befallen him. The business failed, the stock market fell, and his wife left him. As the boils rose under his skin, his hair began to fall out of his scalp. So, in desperation, he went to the top of a mountain and cried out: "Why, God? Why me, God? Please tell me the reason for all of these terrible things being poured out on me!"

As his pitiful cries died out, the clouds parted. A deep, thunderous voice answered from the skies: "Because you bug me!"

Maybe that's exactly how you feel. Maybe you're convinced that every bad thing comes upon you because God doesn't like you. Perhaps you feel there is something fundamentally wrong with you. Therefore, in your search for answers and solace, you tend to turn in upon yourself.

Let's face the facts. We constantly live out of our emotional needs. One of the most powerful needs is to feel loved and accepted as we are. The more subtle and unconscious these psychological needs are, the more they subvert our sense of balance.

Pain serves to intensify what is hidden in us. Physical pain has a diabolical tendency to warp and twist our thinking until we lose the ability to distinguish between what we actually need and what we passionately want. When I'm hurting my mind blurs all other considerations and everything in me focuses on one thought: *I want it to stop.* That desire leads me to turn inward into such introspection that all perspective is lost. If my pain does not stop immediately I wander off the path of perspective into the maze of suffering and turn in upon myself. "God doesn't like me. There is something wrong with me." I have lost sight of God's larger purpose.

I have come to a frightening realization: I am a terribly self-centered person! When given the opportunity, I always try to rearrange the world to fit my needs and wants! When my personal desires are turned aside or when my immediate needs are not met, I become very angry. Then deep anxieties are created within me.

So, here again, in my prayers I may be asking God to grant everything I want. My egotism wants Him to reach out and give a divine stamp of approval to all my prayers. And I want the answer *right now!* When my "wants" aren't fulfilled I see only one possible conclusion: God failed to keep His word! Immediately I am hopelessly confused about what I believe the Bible promises and what *is not* happening through my prayers.

Fortunately into my confusion brother Peter stealthily creeps with his word of wisdom: "These trials are only to test your faith." Quit looking *at* yourself and start looking *to* what could happen. God has larger purposes afoot.

Just changing the habit of thinking only about yourself to something beyond you helps, but what is more helpful is to begin to consider what bigger purposes might be waiting beyond the present moment. The final answers are not in you anyway, so chronic introspection never accomplishes anything.

Recently a friend shared with me how limiting the introspective view can be. At the time, Janet was trapped in an impossible marriage. She was married to an unstable man who was slowly but surely undermining her self-worth and emotional stability. Yet divorce was totally unthinkable for her. She was the mother of two small children. One child had been seriously afflicted by a childhood disease and required constant attention.

What could she do? How could she raise her children by herself? Each question became just another part of an endless circle. Yet as she prayed God seemed to be deaf. He didn't change Janet's husband. There was no indication that He was going to intervene to redeem her marriage. He didn't care! He didn't like her! Engulfed in fear and dread, Janet took matters into her own hands, packed up her belongings and children and left her husband. Ultimately she even had to move to another part of the country.

But Janet was telling me this story more than 15 years later. Now in retrospect she could say, "That divorce was one of the most important things in my life. If I had stayed, we would have all gone down together. At the time I felt God was completely ignoring my pleas. But now I see He was working a plan that was better than anything I could have imagined."

Yes, God's purposes are bigger and better than anything you can ask for in this present moment. Therefore, in His great love and mercy, He will not settle for the little solutions you demand in your self-centered prayers. Just wait. Even when you can't see any possibility, believe that His purposes are at work. Stop looking to yourself. Believe in what is beyond you.

Envision your Christian faith as a strainer through which you can filter all of your life's experiences. Even though you may be pouring in confusion, doubt and perplexity, slowly but surely all your consternation is being screened through God's intentions for your future. When your "wants" are strained through the fabric of God's larger truths, then what is real will precipitate out.

Take the Long View

When we are threatened and afraid we want immediate results! The next five minutes or five hours is everything. The now seems to swallow the future. So our perspective is narrowed to the infinitesimal speck of the next second and the next breath.

When the miracle does not come, we get the feeling that perhaps there will be no future. Oh, life will go on, but living can never be the same again. Time has stopped and at that point we tend to lose our balance.

In contrast, Peter urged that we look to the future. The current problem should be kept in the light of "the day of His return." I personally would translate 1 Peter 1:5: "God's purposes are keeping guard over us for a salvation that won't be completely entire until tomorrow." The future is ahead.

So, the third principle for keeping perspective is to take the long view. The complete purpose of today's problems is known only when tomorrow arrives. When the sun rises again, the shadow will disappear.

What a difference this fuller view makes! It denies that this little dot on the scale of time that we call "now" is everything. It places today against the enormously larger scheme of God's purposes, and what God is doing is never fully or completely known until "the final analysis" is made.

The long view is unfolded in parable form in the movie version of Tolstoy's immortal novel, *War and Peace*. During a scene on the night before the great battle with the French, Prince Andre is studying the battle strategy for the coming day. The Czar is listening and rearranging the maps. Andre asks, "Will we win the battle tomorrow?"

The Czar responds abruptly, "I think not."

The young prince is alarmed. His voice becomes frantic: "Lose the battle! But what if we *do* lose this battle? What will become of us?"

The sage wisdom of the old monarch has a seasoned perspective. "We don't count the battles. We only count the last battle. The last battle is the only one that really matters." He had the present moment in perspective.

God alone holds the key to the final battle and the final battle is what counts most. As Peter said: "For a little while you may have to suffer various trials, so that the genuineness of your faith, . . . may redound to praise and glory and honor" (1 Pet. 1:6,7, *RSV*). The strength of God is akin to patience, not impetuousness. And, His is strength that will win our final battle!

Getting the "tomorrow perspective" placed squarely in the fore of your thinking and feeling will revolutionize your grip on any problem. You can push back the suffocating narrowness of the "now" and open up new avenues to "then."

Remember, God's purposes have enormous leverage! Are you aware of God's laws of leverage that physicists use? These principles allow anybody to move almost anything. Scientists have even postulated that if a long enough lever with a fixed fulcrum point was extended into space, the earth could be pried right out of orbit! Nothing can resist these laws of strength. And God's spiritual laws are no different.

Though the cross of Christ happened in the past, like an enormous lever, its purposes extend into the future. And the fulcrum point is always fixed in today. Today's impossible situation becomes simply the pivot point used to accomplish tomorrow's objectives. Silently and unseen, the awesome leverage of God changes the pattern of history.

Jim Elliot knew this was true. So he began praying for an Auca Indian tribe no one had contacted without being killed. After years of preparation for work as a Wycliffe Bible translator, he and five associates flew into the Amazon jungle to bring the gospel to these remote Indians. They left on January 5, 1956 and disappeared. Five days later the radio report came back to Elizabeth Elliot, Marge Saint and the other wives of these missionaries that all five men had been killed by these primitive warriors.

But God's leverage was not impaired. Through the

years, the writing of Elizabeth Elliot has unfolded the incredible continuing story of that trip. She and the other missionary wives continued to pursue the vision and calling of their husbands. And slowly, like an orchid unfolding from its sheath, those Auca Indians have become Christians. Recently, Marge Saint returned to America with one of the men who had killed the first missionaries. He is now a Christian and anxious to share his faith with America!

Certainly the date of January 5, 1956 is a rock that will not move in the memory of those families. Yet it became the fulcrum point for God's leverage that has moved and affected the world more than 20 years later.

Yes, we can regain our perspective if we realize that even in our suffering we could be standing now at the center of where Christ's cross reaches from today into tomorrow. And of course, that is always a mercy point.

God's Silence Is Never Empty

When you find your emotional balance, avoid chronic introspection and take the long view, several insights become possible. Silence *does not* equate with absence. Far from being indifferent, God intervenes with purposes that are much larger than this present moment only. So I can trust that when nothing divine happens immediately, larger plans are under way. And I won't understand the whole design until I enter tomorrow.

Delay, then, is one part of God's filter system. Silence is a portion of His strategy. While we wait, He is doing important work to us, on the problem, and for others.

Hannah's story conveys such a message. This Old Testament woman longed for a son more than anything in the world. Her husband, Elkanah, loved her more than his other wife. Yet, Hannah could not have children, while Elkanah's other wife had "sons and daugh-

50

ters" which rubbed Hannah's life raw. So she began to pray for a son. The Bible describes her anguish over God's silence in poignant words: "And it happened year after year, as often as she went up to the house of the Lord" (1 Sam. 1:7).

But each of those years Hannah redefined her prayer and redirected her search until her inner life was sensitized so that she could be of very important use in God's plan for all of Israel. In the beginning Hannah came asking only for herself. In the end, God answered for the nation.

So, finally, after her dreams and plans had been thoroughly filtered, she prayed: "O Lord of hosts, if Thou wilt indeed look on the affliction of Thy maidservant and . . . wilt give Thy maidservant a son, then I will give him to the Lord all the days of his life" (1 Sam. 1:11). And shortly thereafter Samuel was born. The following years of Israel's history revolved around the personality of this giant. But the years of God's silence were essential preparation for Samuel's birth.

Without the times of God's silence your life would be deprived of its greater influence. You would grow less if God intervened dramatically and immediately in your times of trouble.

Difficulty Produces Diamonds, Gold and Butterflies

Only the hottest heat and the greatest pressure have sufficient force to change black, worthless carbon into sparkling diamonds of immense value; and millions of years are required for the process to be complete. As the hottest fire makes the finest gems, so the most painful problems shape the most mature life. A priceless character is not formed overnight.

True, fire will also burn. Tragedy and calamity can shrivel and shrink our lives. These times of trouble can

51

embitter and stunt every good emotion. However, nothing can flaw your personality unless you allow it. *The problem isn't in what happens to you but on how you take it.*

Right now, determine that you will turn your difficulties into diamonds. You will *not* let despair rob you of your priceless jewels. You *will* receive your problems with the positive expectation that they will perfect your life and faith. Peter had this very idea in mind when he described our trials as existing for the purification of our faith (see 1 Pet. 1:6,7).

Gold is refined by fire. We can be, too. In the midst of the heat, the hidden voice of God might usher forth, as it did in Moses' experience with the burning bush. Most of us just don't stay long enough to hear Him speak.

Waiting in the midst of fire until God can be seen and heard melts away the slag and residue of your trials. What seems worthless and unnecessary can result in purification and perfection.

The caterpillar's necessary metamorphosis into a glistening butterfly demands he spin himself into a cocoon. Once the brown capsule is finished nothing must touch it. When the newly formed butterfly starts to emerge, he must struggle and fight to push himself free. If there is any help from the outside, the little creature will never fly. Only through the agony and struggle of cracking the cocoon, can the Monarch's wings spread.

If God uses struggle to transform such an insignificant source of beauty, would He keep us from anything less that will complete our personhood? Our painful experiences that close around us like a tomb, become the mold in which our wings are formed. What seems to be so hindering may be the very strength that allows us to fly. These times of silence from God may be the times we are completing our personhood. No matter what the trial may be, our pain can forge new dimensions of life and vitality.

Paul agreed with Peter about the prospects. He wrote, "I reckon that the sufferings of this present time are not worthy to be compared with the glory which shall be revealed in us" (Rom. 8:18, *KJV*). Anticipating such a fulfilling future will definitely develop a glad heart.

Do these suggestions work? Can such a faith really make a difference? It all depends on your perspective.

As we were eating in a local restaurant with Mary and her husband, the waitress somehow got into the conversation. Though rather dumbfounded, we found ourselves listening to her tale of woe. Actually not a lot that had happened to her was either really dramatically good or bad, but she seemed to feel tragedy was waiting for her at every corner.

She ended by saying, "Well, I'm a Capricorn and I guess that's why I've had such a hard life." And off she went to afflict the people at the next table.

With a sigh of relief we went back to finishing the dessert. But Mary added her own afterthought. "Well, people do believe in the silliest things. I'm a Capricorn and I certainly haven't had a tragic life."

Her quiet words came through with magnificent force. From her perspective, her life had not been filled with hard things. Yet, this child of poor dust-bowl farmers had lived for years with the most agonizing problems possible. Her first child was born deaf and with a withered hand. He required constant care until he finally died of a brain tumor at five years of age. Her second child nearly died. And the suspected genetic flaw that caused these problems prevented Mary and her husband from having other children.

But Mary couldn't remember having a hard life! Out

53

of her own relationship with Christ had come a glad heart. Her strong emotional balance allowed her to discover God, working through every experience in her life. Her emotional balance and trusting faith made a world of difference for her.

Some Concluding Thoughts

Hurting throws our emotions off balance. Our eyes tend to perceive only what we feel. And the result can bring despair. When nothing tangible develops from our prayers, we often conclude God is gone. That conclusion just isn't true!

We must press on to discover what our heavenly Father is doing. To begin an inquiry into the deeper ways of God demands that we seek a balanced frame of mind. We must look for a larger perspective into which we can set our hurts.

You cannot have insight if you are completely tied in knots from extreme introspection. So get your eyes off of yourself and recognize that your emotions can deceive. Turn your focus toward the message that God's mercy is constant. Start over with a renewed confidence that God is always present and is at work right now.

How can I be so certain God is really concerned and aware of me even in the silence? Jesus Christ is my personal assurance that the heavenly Father is holding the torn pieces of my life. So by studying the pattern of Jesus' life and ministry, I find clues to help me recognize that God is still working. And Jesus has shown me that silence is in itself a strategy. My willingness to allow God to accomplish long-range goals may finally bring far more dramatic results than would occur from an immediate miraculous intervention.

When there is no miracle, I need to know that God also speaks through silence. Because of Jesus, I know the silence is not empty. God labors in the shadows.

Some Questions to Ponder

1. Think back to a time when you prayed for help during a hard situation. Did God answer your prayer the way you wanted Him to? Or did He turn a "deaf ear" to your plea? What was the outcome of the situation? Can you see why God answered the way He did? Can you see that God has answered your prayer, in any way?

2. When there seems to be no answer to your prayers, do you assume it's all your fault? How does God's silence make you feel about yourself? Your faithfulness? How could your feelings be misleading you?

3. Do you think Jesus was being "introspective" when He called to His Father from the cross in Matthew 27:46? When God doesn't relieve you of pain—emotional or physical—do you feel like He doesn't like you anymore or that there is something wrong with your faith? What does Romans 8:38,39 say about God's love?

4. Try to take the long view if you are going through a hard situation now. Imagine some ways that God might answer your prayer. What changes might He be making in your life by letting you struggle for a period of time?

three

A Personal Conversation with Jesus_____

"Dear Jesus, I think a terrible mistake was made in how the world was created."

"A mistake? You think the heavenly Father makes mistakes?" Jesus' reply was quick and with just a touch of amusement.

But having seen the cruelty of life I knew something in creation was more than wrong. Surely, there must be some fatal flaw running through everything.

"I think an error was made in making us like we are. Really, Jesus, couldn't things have been made differently?"

"You must understand the heavenly Father is not afraid of the excesses of men nor is He dismayed by the storm." Jesus spoke with a deliberate tone. "What if the rains do consume the crops and the floods fill the valleys?"

Frankly I could think of nothing but harm that could result. But Jesus continued with another question.

"Do the crops never grow again? Or does the fertile plain receive new soil that gives back a crop of a hundred-fold more yield? So even men with evil intent only furnish a seedbed for other days and times to bring forth an unexpected harvest of good. Though problems do happen, the Father intends only the best for His creation. But these hard things are allowed because He does redeem even the worst the world has to give."

The
Paradox
of
PAIN

On December 7, 1941, without warning, hundreds of people were killed by the bombs that fell on the Island of Oahu. Aboard the fleet anchored in the bay were many young Navy boys dreaming of future careers and their girl friends back home. Seemingly without provocation, hordes of Japanese fell on their helpless prey.

Like angry vultures devouring flesh and muscle, they forever crushed the dreams and hopes of countless families. In a matter of moments, sons and fathers melted together in the waves of fire that fell from the skies. The ashes of smoldering airplanes and sinking battleships bore their own mute testimony to the unstoppable attack. As the sun set that evening, light died out on the hopes and dreams of a generation of Americans.

On December 8, a minister was stopped on the street by a blurry-eyed parishioner. The broken man whose son had sunk with one of those battleships clutched at the minister's sleeve. His grip had the feel of belligerence that implied blame. His trembling hand almost conveyed threat of retaliation. But his cracking voice betrayed the inner mixture of anguish and anger.

"What kind of a God did this? If your God could have stopped this and didn't, He must be a terrible God! And if He couldn't have prevented it, He isn't worth the time of day!"

Such agony shatters easy answers as surely as bombs shatter the unprotected. Approximately four years later the same dilemma was forced on the enemy.

At another island in the Pacific, in an industrial city called Hiroshima, the sky turned red and the moon to blood. As the all-engulfing mushroom cloud swallowed everything in its path, the tables turned. In the instant in which the first atom bomb was detonated, the same terrible questions were etched again in history.

Have we forgotten those early pictures of children with their eyes sealed shut from the heat which seared everything in its path? To this day men and women bear scars of burns where whole patches of skin dissolved like melting butter. Most families were unable to recover even the remains of their loved ones. They just vanished in that dreadful puff of smoke.

What sort of God would let men loose to create such weapons of holocaust? Devouring locusts at least leave the roots to sprout again. But mankind's destruction even contaminates the soil and the future.

Why has God allowed us to do these monstrous things?

Can We Make Allowance?

Our problem is in the word "allow." The terrible things that God allows in this world make us worry

59

about what He is really like and whether He does anything directly. So far, I have argued that God *does* work even during the awful times. Yet, *how* does God bring creative results while all of these terrible things still happen? We must find further insight into the usefulness of our conflicts.

Further, these calamities make us wonder about the effectiveness of God's power. I can truly identify with the man who lost his son at Pearl Harbor whenever my family or my body is touched. At those moments I want to know exactly *how* God works.

Let's look at an incident in the ministry of Jesus where an affliction existed from birth and yet a miracle also happened. The story began as the disciples and Jesus encountered a man born blind.

> "Rabbi, who sinned, this man or his parents, that he should be born blind?" Jesus answered, "It was neither that this man sinned, nor his parents; but it was in order that the works of God might be displayed in him. We must work the works of Him who sent Me, as long as it is day; night is coming, when no man can work. While I am in the world, I am the light of the world. "... He spat on the ground and made clay of the spittle, and applied the clay to his eyes, and said to him, "Go, wash in the pool of Siloam" (which is translated, Sent). And so he went away and washed, and came back seeing (John 9:2-7).

That's an exciting story! However, the point is not to confound us with the miracle of a man receiving his sight, but to demonstrate who Jesus is. The blindness became the further opportunity Jesus used to announce to the community that the Messiah had come. The blindness was not the result of anyone's sin or a cause for blame or a comment on the man's faith or integrity. In fact, Jesus doesn't actually explain why the condition existed. But the disability was allowed to exist so that, at the very moment of Jesus' passing, the condition would be worked into God's grand design.

Can't you hear the content of the blind man's conversations with his parents through the years? "Why is there no miracle? Why doesn't God give me sight?"

And the parents try to comfort him with phrases like, "Son, be patient and trust God. He will not forget you. Someday He will touch your life."

All those words must have sounded trite and contrived until that afternoon when Jesus came by. But we've given the same type of assurances because we didn't know what else to say. Yet, in the last analysis, those are powerful sentences of faith.

God can afford to allow a world riddled with inconsistencies. At the right time the works of God are manifest. The lack of a miracle is only a signal that the time is not ripe and that God's best moment is not yet ready to be fulfilled.

So, let's build on one of the principles for perspective that we discovered in chapter 2. The Russian Czar taught us that real power is the ability to win the last battle. True strength can concede an immediate skirmish to obtain a final objective.

Here's another dimension of that point: *Power is the ability to achieve a purpose.*

Let the weight of that sink in for a few moments because the definition is contrary to popular usage. Most of the time we think of power as being synonomous with sheer force, unleashed brute might. Our minds conjure up words like *violent* and *explosive.* I get mental pictures of houses being blown into a thousand splinters. Or, I see a football player tackled with such animal zest that as he flies backwards his helmet rips loose, his head smashes into the turf and the ball bursts free. That's force! We enjoy the sense of seeming omnipotence that such usage conveys to us. Brute strength dashes barriers to the ground!

But these mental pictures are misleading. Born out of adolescent desires, our fantasies lack the maturity to grasp the fuller meaning of true power—the ability to restrain in order to accomplish the greater gain. When we talk of the ability to delay in order to accomplish larger purposes, we have entered the realm of God's power.

A more adequate image is found in the scenic landscape of Hoover Dam. The dam could let loose a torrent of water that would cut through the canyon with blinding devastation, crumpling houses like waste paper. Any creature in the path of that wall of water would vanish beneath a sea of mud. But the aftermath would not be a demonstration of the true power.

The power of that retainer is in its ability to restrain those countless gallons of water and to release them in controlled amounts. The ability to use pressure for creative production is the true measure of the dam's real strength. Power is demonstrated in the purposefulness of an action.

This is the clue we need to understand how God's power operates and why such contradictory conditions are allowed to happen in our world. Nothing can keep the purposes of God from being manifest. His true strength can wait its time until the best minute has come. No miracle? No intervention by God? Remember that is only a commentary on the past. The future is wide open with possibility!

So let's look at three floodgates God uses to enter tomorrow. These three truths help us understand God's restraint in selecting the proper time to accomplish the most good. Even His restraint is a part of His future for us.

Ruins Can Be Recast

No miracle! Nothing more happened! And even worse, everything just blew apart! Well, what of these purposes of God when our dreams are scattered over the hillside like broken pieces of pottery?

Even a great prophet like Isaiah struggled to understand how God did things. He wrestled with the fact that the Lord God of Israel would allow His chosen people to fall and be dragged through the dust by a heathen nation. The ignominy and the tragedy of the people of God defeated and in exile was almost more than his mind could grasp. Maybe God was inept?

And equally perplexing was his prophetic insight that a foreign and enemy king would be used to bring the children of Israel out of bondage. How could God put His hand on Cyrus of Persia to serve as His annointed representative? For the Jews, such a thought seemed to conflict with all that God said He would allow. So, what could the prophet say?

Isaiah found his answer in the village potter when his eye caught the fascinating spin of the wheel. Watching the clay turn and the sure hands of the potter shape and mold, he discovered how real power works. Many times the potter worked and twisted and formed the unyielding lump before his hands achieved the desired shape—the clay's ultimate destiny. Yet, the potter patiently held fast until his design was accomplished.

So God spoke to Isaiah's question: "Woe to the one who quarrels with his Maker—An earthenware vessel

63

among the vessels of earth! Will the clay say to the potter, 'What are you doing?' " (Isa. 45:9).

No, the clay remains ready for whatever the potter's hand intends to fashion. And should a problem occur, there is a procedure already at work to correct any fault in the design. The ruined can always be recast. Imperfection is allowable because in the end it will be reworked into the completed object. And in the end something much better will be produced.

Paul picked up on this theme in almost the identical words of Isaiah:

> The thing molded will not say to the molder, "Why did you make me like this," will it? Or does not the potter have a right over the clay, to make from the same lump one vessel for honorable use, and another for common use? What if God, although willing to demonstrate His wrath and to make His power known, endured with much patience vessels of wrath prepared for destruction? And He did so in order that He might make known the riches of His glory upon vessels of mercy, which He prepared beforehand for glory (Rom. 9:20-23).

The apostle's concern was to explain why the Jewish people had been set aside in God's plan. After coming through all the calamity, now the Gentiles were receiving God's Gift. So Jews asked, "Was God's power really working in all of our upheavals?"

And the same answer comes again. Absolutely! And now God has recast the results so that the world will be blessed. The skill of the potter is not demonstrated when he pulls the clay apart and hurls the mud at the wall. The ultimate power of the artist is displayed when the broken pieces are reshaped into a new result. So with gentleness, God's fingers wait with the right pressure to accomplish the correct result. And God recast Israel's sufferings and failures into the salvation of the world! Something bigger and better came out of the pieces.

Can God do that with us today? Yes! In fact, He is doing this all the time! Have you read the story of Maria Anne Hirschman? She shares her life in *Hansi, The Girl Who Loved The Swastika*. Maria's life is one continuous example of how in God's perfect timing the ruins are recast. First, her mother died leaving her an orphan to be raised in a poor peasant home in Czechoslovakia. But the foster mother's love pointed her to Christ. Then as a talented teenager she was chosen to be trained as a Nazi youth leader.

The Third Reich stripped her of her Christian faith. So when Germany fell her entire world crashed. She was captured and sent to a communist work camp. But even through all these circumstances the Potter's wheel was turning. She escaped to a whole new future in America. Through the seemingly empty years the Father's hand was never slack in remolding an orphan child into an instrument of His grace. Today countless numbers of Americans have been challenged by her messages.

The Nazis would have formed a vessel of wrath. But God could wait. In His timing, out of the riches of His glory He shaped a vessel of mercy named Hansi!

Can God do that with you right now? Indeed, He already is! Don't struggle with questions like, "What are you making, God?" Be secure in knowing that every ruin can be recast.

Everything Is Usable
Even as a potter casts the waste clay back into the

lump to be molded, God uses everything that happens to us in creating His final work in our lives. The heavenly Father can allow seemingly unrelated events to happen to us, that do not reflect His intentions for us, because He can redeem anything. When He is through working there are no leftovers!

Isn't that an amazing paradox? While our hardest moments are not sent by God, He still can pick them up and use them in a new and constructive pattern. Can you believe He works this way? Can you trust this second procedure God uses? Many people can't! For them the mere fact of suffering is a complete contradiction of God's goodness.

Archibald MacLeish tackled this question in his play *J.B.* His modern parody on the book of Job placed J.B. and his family in a contemporary setting. To keep the ancient dilemma before us, MacLeish introduced a rhyme:

> If God is Will
> And Will is well
> Then what is ill?
> God still?
> Dew tell![1]

MacLeish's problem is in understanding *how* God's power operates. There would seem to be a contradiction between believing that God is all-powerful and all-loving, and yet He still allows the painful times. In personal terms we wonder, "If He is totally in control, and completely loves me, then why doesn't He intervene this instant?"

So we need to understand how God accomplishes His purposes. Remember, I said power is demonstrated in the purposefulness of an action. So let's inquire further into how restraint is the very hallmark of God's complete control.

C.S. Lewis has keen insight into how the eternal intentions are accomplished. In his book, *The Problem of Pain*, he has written a brilliant chapter on the meaning of God's omnipotence.

The Oxford don notes that we let ourselves fall into a grammatical trap. Our confusion comes from defining omnipotence as "the ability to do the impossible." We are quite fond of saying God is the God of the impossible! Certainly that has a great sound. But the affirmation carries an inherent contradiction.

What we mean is that God can do what isn't possible for men to accomplish. Or, we may be implying that God can act under conditions which are not open to us. Often the hidden implication is that the need cannot be met "unless" an unseen ingredient is added. But with popular usage the word "impossible" slips away from us and comes to say something very different.

The word gets over into the world of magicians. "Impossible" takes on the cloak of the trickster who seems to make flowers appear out of the air. ("Impossible" seems to be what we see on television when the camera is doing trick photography.) We lose sight of the logical explanations for all of the effects. There is no magic. Rather, we just don't have the facts only the magician sees. So, we use "impossible" to stand for self-contradictory actions. In reality there is no such thing!

So what does "impossible" mean? Exactly what the word says. It is not possible! A particular action or situation is intrinsically not a reality. The dictionary defines the word as "not capable of existing or happening." To speak of something or some action as being impossible is to say such an event or idea is self-contradictory.

So Dr. Lewis clarifies the matter:

> His Omnipotence means power to do all that
> is intrinsically possible, not to do the intrinsi-
> cally impossible. You may attribute miracles
> to Him, but not nonsense. This is no limit to
> His power. If you choose to say "God can give
> a creature free will and at the same time with-
> hold free will from it," you have not succeed-
> ed in saying *anything* about God: meaning-
> less combinations of words do not suddenly
> acquire meaning simply because we prefix to
> them the two other words "God can." It re-
> mains true that all *things* are possible with
> God: the intrinsic impossibilities are not
> things but nonentities. It is no more possible
> for God than for the weakest of His creatures
> to carry out both of two mutually exclusive
> alternatives; not because His power meets an
> obstacle, but because nonsense remains non-
> sense even when we talk it about God.[2]

Are you beginning to get a feel of what we do so often
in our sermons and prayers? In our enthusiasm we sub-
tly talk ourselves into ideas that have nothing at all to
do with the way God is. So, what happens when the
prayer can't be answered? Our disappointment is similar
to discovering there is no real Santa Claus to come down
the chimney.

Yes, we can pray asking God to do everything that is
intrinsically possible and in accord with His purposes.
But to search for divine blessing for "mutually exclu-
sive" situations leads to a dead-end street.

Nevertheless, God keeps right on working regardless
of the alternatives. And He can and does redeem the

broken pieces of your world. Everything in your life is usable to Him.

The World Can Be Used "As Is"

God doesn't have to overrule the world to accomplish His results. Dramatic interventions that overrule nature's laws aren't necessary for God's work to be done anyway.

True, there are some real problems in what God has allowed. If we are given the ability to discover radium and atomic energy, we also have the potential to blow up the world. When He chose to give us the intelligence to discover fire He also gave us the freedom to burn down the forest. God is really bound by His choices and human freedom is part of this.

And, of course, this misuse of our freedom is a paradox also. The suffering which men inflict on each other is not a failure of God's power, but the abuse of our opportunities. So the greater the opportunity God has given to us, the worse will be the perversion. When love is twisted, it becomes hate; fallen innocence produces the worst depravity.

But God can allow such a world as ours. In the face of potential perversion, His restraint is still purposeful. Even this fallen creation can be used just as it is.

And what does this procedure have to do with you when there is no miracle? What meaning does the restraint of God have when you bump your head? Well, reflect back on what happened with your first pair of roller skates. I recall best the feel of the concrete sidewalk. Oh, did that hurt!

So, when my daughter, the apple of my eye, wanted skates I had considerable apprehension. Those lovely little knees didn't need the experience I had acquired years before. Moreover, she could break an arm or leg.

No, I just didn't want to allow a potential fall.

Traci explained the situation to me. "Daddy, I can't ever learn to stay up if I don't fall down a little bit." True, that's the way God always is.

Love knows growing up and maturing means allowing the possibility of falling down. We would never learn to care without going through hurt's door. Our children must be allowed many hard experiences we would never intend if they would become competent adults. We can't expect the love of God to be less.

My two oldest boys have always been more like twins. Being less than a year apart and almost the same size, they have had a fierce rivalry at times. When they were in grade school we were very disappointed because of their fighting.

My wife feared they would kill each other! Todd and Tony had bloody noses, black eyes and split lips. None of this was our intention. Our dream of two loving little boys seemed as impossible as having clean hand towels in the house.

Recently I asked my older boy if he would like to take a ski trip with a group of Young Lifers. Now that Todd's grown to 16, I felt he could handle an extended trip away from home. He asked if Tony was going.

Since Tony had a job the trip wouldn't be possible. Todd thought about it a moment and replied, "I don't think I'd enjoy skiing much without him."

At least two minutes passed as I absorbed that response. From raw knuckles to real companionship. Where had the change happened? Of course, lots of growth and maturity were reflected in those few words. Somewhere in allowing two boys to get close enough to clobber each other, caring had come through. This is a symbol of how restraint and time are used to create results that dramatic intervention could never bring.

What a paradox!

Pain is not something God intends for us. But He allows us the opportunity so that the greater objectives will be accomplished. Life is used "as is."

Power and love are not two extremes that stand in contrast to each other. God's omnipotence and constant caring never are in contradiction. Rather, they complement each other. They are as continuous circles that surround everything that happens to us. We are always surrounded by God's circle of caring.

Some Concluding Thoughts

The times of silence are not an affront to our faith, our hopes, nor our self-worth. We don't have to cower in the shadows, ensnared by guilt. The delay in an immediate miracle doesn't imply a divine comment on our sinfulness, nor is it a judgment on our ability to truly believe.

Rather, a great paradox is at work! While God doesn't send tragedy, He still allows it; then He takes and re-shapes everything that happens to us. And as a potter forms a large lump of clay, God uses our experiences as they come.

How does God work so quietly? Though floods, famines, fires consume everything good in their path, God still sustains His universe. In the end, the world is only swept clean for lush green growth and greater harvest. And the heavenly Father is doing the same with you.

When there is no miracle, I've learned not to doubt His intentions and power; I can trust God to achieve His purposes in a more conventional manner. While I cannot see the fullness of the plan at this point, I know the Potter's wheel has begun to spin again.

If your life is cracked through to the very core, start listening intently. Somewhere in the background the wheel has already started to move. Right now, begin to look for the new thing being shaped by the unseen hand. Open yourself for possibilities you otherwise wouldn't even consider. Why not lay the broken pieces on the table before Him? Could you dare to have your life reassembled purely as *He* chooses?

Some Questions to Ponder

1. Can you accept this statement: "The lack of a miracle is only a signal that the time is not ripe and that God's best moment is not yet ready to be fulfilled?" Do you believe this has happened in your life or is happening right now?

2. What does C.S. Lewis mean when he says that God, the Omnipotent, cannot do the "intrinsically impossible?" How does this statement affect your own definition of a miracle? Have you prayed for "impossible" things?

3. Can you visualize God as a Potter, taking everything that happens to you and molding these events into a meaningful, completely fulfilling destiny, that only He knows about? How, then, does this affect your prayer life?

4. If God is all-loving how can He allow so much evil and pain in the world? Review the section "The World Can Be Used 'As Is.'"

5. How does the cross of Christ demonstrate that God is, at the same time, all-powerful and all-loving?

Notes

1. Archibald MacLeish, *J.B.* (Cambridge, Mass.: The Riverside Press, 1956), p. 78.
2. C.S. Lewis, *The Problem of Pain* (New York: The Macmillan Company, 1962), p. 28.

four

By this time I had come to realize how difficult His road might become. The cost had grown as His teaching continued. "Isn't there another path we can take?"

And Jesus stared at me with an intensity I had not yet seen. My carefully made plans seemed to be devoured by that look.

"Would you be with me wherever I am?"

My reply was immediate, "Oh, of course, Master, always!"

"Then let us arise and go out to the place where men are naked. Tonight, we must share the bread of starving people."

"Jesus, I don't think I want to go. You and your words are what I long to have."

"Then you must understand my meaning. You cannot have me without my other friends."

The Profit from PAIN

Profit from pain? Well, we've found some reasons to give us more than stoic resolution. Maybe we have even begun to find a new inner flow of meaning that is truly sustaining. But are we really at the place where we can affirm and believe that our suffering could be truly profitable?

That was my question as I listened to Susie share the story of her last few months with John. Early in their life they had acquired many of the good things most people strive after for decades. Young, with beautiful children, nothing could stifle their abundance. Nothing! Nothing except the final diagnosis that John had cancer of the spine.

Slowly, painfully, completely, the specter of death crept into their lives. At first it was only an irritation. Then the limp appeared; next the leg began to drag. The wheelchair was only the prelude to incapacitation in bed. Though the enemy moved only by degrees, he never retreated and his inch-by-inch conquest was final.

John's last Christmas with his family was bicycle time. The children were thrilled and excited to demonstrate their skill and tricks. Up and down in front of the house roared the racers. Susie wheeled John to the window to watch their performance. Once he was in place, the children had the only audience that counted. But as John sat in the shadows tears trickled down his face. At his side Susie stood helpless. His pains and remorse were compounded for her as she not only felt his suffering but found her pain multiplied by the knowledge of his approaching death.

As Susie was telling me this, months after John's death, I asked, "Susie, this must linger with you like a nightmare." I could feel how many other afflicting moments must be hidden in her memory.

"Oh no, I'm grateful. I'm grateful for this chapter in my life. Don't get me wrong. It was a terrible time and the pain will never be completely gone. There's a sense in which things will never be back to normal again. But when I remember all the things God has done in my life I have to use the word grateful. I grew through every minute of John's illness. God used this terrible thing as His opportunity."

The experience of this young widowed mother causes us to begin to calculate the many ways in which our own hard times have brought profit into our lives. When we measure our trials against hers, balance is quickly restored. If after living through a year of daily dying she can find possibilities, hope must be scattered around the rocks over which we have stumbled.

Sorting through my memories, I found a common thread that tied my experiences together with Susie's positive recollections: *Pain shatters our illusions!*

Her insight was absolutely true. Many false ideas crumble under the impact of hurting. Out of the dust of our little plaster ideas about life can arise new refined sensitivity and renewed care.

Invisible shackles of smugness and complacency can bind us down to mediocrity and mundaneness. We don't realize that our thick blinders keep us looking only at the familiar and comfortable side of life. Any profit comes when we rip the hindrances off even when the cost is high.

Like crusty Silas Marner, we creep into our stuffy, snug world of isolation. Perhaps there is more of the old Silas in our indifference than we care to admit. Frighteningly, out of the rut we call our daily path, might we have come to think like an emotional recluse? If so, anything that strips away our artificiality is valuable!

Freedom Issues from Suffering

At the moment of tragedy's impact we can't see that we are being freed to become more sensitive. While the hoped-for miracle still seems possible, our focus is absorbed with matters of survival. Only later can we realize how bound and conditioned we were in those moments before the page was torn from our book. But now maybe we have come to the place where we can realize the freedom that Christ was giving us as we were being sustained in our valley of shadows.

Having discovered something of what God is doing during the silent times, now we can discover *where* He is working. Recognizing where the rough edges are filed, allows us to have greater endurance. Regardless of what happens to our eyesight, our inner vision is being healed. Illusions are being broken.

Certainly, this was the apostle Paul's experience. He

had an almost table-pounding enthusiasm about the value of his suffering. The freedom that hardship had given him was remolded into a vessel that could serve others. Out of the emptiness of his bowl had come a feast for every starving man. Paul, too, could say, "Oh, I'm grateful. I'm grateful for this chapter in my life."

> Thank God, the Father of our Lord Jesus Christ, that he is our Father and the source of all mercy and comfort. For he gives us comfort in our trials so that we in turn may be able to give the same sort of strong sympathy to others in theirs. Indeed, experience shows that the more we share Christ's suffering, the more we are able to give of his encouragement. This means that if we experience trouble we can pass on to you comfort and spiritual help; for if we ourselves have been comforted we know how to encourage you to endure patiently the same sort of troubles that we ourselves have endured. We are quite confident that if you have to suffer troubles as we have done, then, like us, you will find the comfort and encouragement of God. We should like you, our brothers, to know something of what we went through in Asia. At that time we were completely overwhelmed; the burden was more than we could bear; in fact we told ourselves that this was the end. Yet we believe now that we had this experience of coming to the end of our tether that we might learn to trust, not in ourselves, but in God who can raise the dead. It was God who preserved us from imminent death, and it is he who still preserves us. Further, we trust

Him to keep us safe in the future" (2 Cor. 1:3-11, *Phillips*).

Only in coming to death can you personally know for a fact that God does raise the dead! Out of heartbreaking discouragement, comes the certainty of divine encouragement! And only in the bending and breaking of our illusions do we become powerful people of the Spirit like Paul.

If we share in Christ's suffering, we have the potential to be a part of His redemptive work in the world. That means I can dig even a little deeper into my experience and find that some of the greatest possible values hide there.

So what are these places where God is working? We must look at some of the illusions that can be shattered.

And They Lived Happily Ever After

Every middle-class fairy tale ends with this falsely reassuring afterthought. The benevolent god of social assurance covers our hopes with a layer of the finest baloney. Everything is O.K. and life is good. We will all live happily evermore.

Though we have become much more sophisticated than the naïve world of several decades past, the myth still flows in our blood. We may feel avante-garde reading a Camus novel or Elia Kazan's ambiguous doubts. Yet our hearts reside in a different place. Most Americans are insulated from the realities that plague the majority of the world's people.

Why not? Our world is filled with never-ending grocery store counters, adequate heating, and more than sufficient clothing. With central air-conditioning, central heating, and central television, ours is a never-ending circle of ease.

The illusion: *there are no problems on our block.* So we become insulated and rather isolated. And in the end, we turn insipid. That contact with the nuts and bolts of life is so distant that our emotions and compassions rust from lack of use.

And what is reality? Though 2,000 years separate us in time, Paul was much closer to contemporary truth than is this "average" American. The vast majority of the world lives closer to the end of the tether than at the top of the ladder.

Very, very, very few people experience unbroken happiness for any extended period of time. Television, radio, newspapers all scream out the daily pattern of tragedy's surprise visit. Inevitably into every life some rain does fall and for many, living is a continuing monsoon.

I must be forced to look again behind the masks of the countless smiles I meet. Illusions of tranquility must be shattered. Genuine encouragement can be extended only when I know how to recognize the discouragement that is traveling behind the appearance of well-being.

An ancient wise man said, "All progress is bought by pain and all history is paid for in blood." Nothing goes forward without dissatisfaction. Without the hard times I settle for the lowest common denominator.

Because of this, I now have a very different prayer of gratitude:

Thank you Father, that you refuse to let me settle for appearance. I'm grateful that you convict me of lying when I want to act like the unpleasant things aren't there. Thank you for forcing me to see prejudice, callousness and the evil of the world. Sometimes I do have bad dreams. But Father, I'd rather see bad images

79

that are true than to think pleasant thoughts
when men I could help are dying all around
me. In the name of Christ's suffering. Amen.

God never seems to tire of answering my prayer. In
between the asking and the receiving, I am given life in
such large doses I don't have time to let the insulation
corrupt my best motivations.

New sensitivity was thrust on us during one of our
numerous trips to the hospital. Todd was only six years
old when his congenital kidney problem surfaced. The
surgery was rough and the recovery long for such a little
fellow. We found ourselves totally absorbed in comforting him. And we all felt a bit sorry for ourselves. Here
we were having to go through an experience most
people never have.

A distant cry down the hall began interrupting our
reflections. At first we were irritated that our own need
for quiet was being so constantly disrupted. Then we
became insensed that the parents or nurses were obviously not attending some child. After a day of the cre-
scendo of whimpering and wailing, I decided to
investigate the nuisance.

To my horror I found a 13-year-old boy, strapped to
a revolving metal tray. His naked body was stretched
out and belted down like a victim in a medieval torture
chamber. From the back of his neck to his heels swelled
a solid mass of scabs and singed skin. From the open
door I gasped at the sight. Gauze had been pressed into
some of the open skin but other areas appeared open and
angry.

Quietly I closed the door. Standing in the hall I realized that though the cries varied in intensity, the under-
lying pain never diminished. But why was no one in the
room with him?

The answer came quick enough. He and his father had been hit by a gasoline truck running a stop sign. The father died in the flames that charred the teenager. Months before, his mother had died. There was no mother to visit him and no money for a private nurse.

But something could be done. His cries were not so much from pain as from the healing process—skin grafts had begun. This created a pulling sensation that caused intense itching. He was almost being driven mad by the lack of relief. There was no sleep, no reprieve, no peace.

Our own selfish needs and wants shrank quickly. Where we had been irritated, now we had compassion to try to help the boy. Perhaps there was something we could do. Yes, a great deal could be done. If someone with sterilized gloves would gently touch the gauzed areas, relief would be immediate. Given enough minutes of satisfaction the child could go to sleep and begin to compose himself emotionally.

Immediately we began calling some of the high school youth we knew. The situation was explained and shifts of boys were organized to perform the delicate task of easing the irritation. Around the clock teams stood by to bring comfort and companionship. In the sterile lonely room down the hall love was on the way.

What was it like to put on those gloves and touch that hideous back? Some got nauseated and others found it difficult to eat their next meal. No one ever really wanted to do it again. Yet, they came back hour after hour.

Watching the little guy sleep was worth every moment. To hear him begin to make little jokes was pure joy. We had found a better alternative to uninvolved, unconcerned middle-class thinking.

The Alternative: Become Partners with Pain

Our world is full of broken people. Once our illusions

81

of a happy-ever-after are shattered we can help bring wholeness to others. And that will do an immensely important thing to us. Like a seed cracking open, a new sprout of life will arise in us. A new concern, a new sensitivity, a new variety of love will start to leaf out and flower. No longer can we be introverted and inept. We are surrounded by too many people crying out for our cup of cold water to ever let our inner spring go stale.

As we try to fill empty cups a second realization will develop in our consciousness. We begin to see how utterly helpless we are to really make any lasting significant changes. One of our most important discoveries is recognizing how enormous are our limitations.

With bravado we decide to fight the dragons. Inevitably, we are humbled to discover they are legion. With our first burst of dedication we know we can change the world. But we will be forced to realize very little is possible unless we are in partnership with God.

The disillusionment with our own abilities is, perhaps, the most valuable breakthrough of all. Being humbled by the size of the task changes us from being "do-gooders" to becoming tools of the Father. After we are split open to the center of our soul, we are ready to pray the type of prayer that counts. Catherine Marshall helped me frame my experience in what she calls her "prayer of helplessness." She wrote:

> God has never allowed me the fulfillment of a soul's desire without first putting me through an acute realization of my own inadequacy, and my need for help. It shouldn't surprise us that creativity arises out of the pit of life rather than the high places. For creativity is the ability to put old material into new form. And it is only when old molds

and old ways of doing things are forcibly broken up by need or suffering, compelling us to regroup, to rethink, to begin again, that the creative process starts to flow.[1]

Only in coming to my inadequacy am I able to catch sight of the inexhaustible sufficiency of God. As I get rid of the foolish happy-ever-after notions, I am able to pass on not *my* encouragement but *His* strong encouragement. The new creativity that begins to pulsate in my veins makes the price worth any recompense.

I Don't Need Nobody!

Consider another illusion. The James Cagney tough guy is amusing to watch. With his shoulder holster and big cigar he tells the world, "I don't need nobody—see!" Many of us are Cagney caricatures. We may be much more subtle but we are just as independent.

This second major illusion is where God goes to work on our sense of total self-sufficiency. On the gut level we're not sure that we really need anybody. We visualize the main street of the world running right in front of our house. The axis of the globe turns on what happens in our living room. And the result is the conviction that we can make it by ourselves. God ought to feel lucky to have us playing on His team.

My world has always been filled with rugged individualists. We're westerners! Our relatives either came in covered wagons or were here in teepees. Many Oklahomans are truly the sons of the pioneers. Once we get our boots on, we can wipe out anything that rides in!

Of course, we're not sure how God fits into all this. Our rugged individualism seems to have a hard time accepting Deity. And we're really not so different from what is happening with the vast majority of secular society; only the settings change. The attitude is the same. God doesn't fit into our fundamental desire "to do it my way."

God is, for many, no more than an interpretation for what isn't explained by any other data. What is not covered by our experience is just interpreted by the word, G-O-D. There's nothing personal about the matter. But using that word helps if our understanding gets a little weak.

Or, God may simply be an interruption. In some way He gets involved in some of our more base natural tendencies and makes us feel guilty. The result is that basically He is a bother.

Though we wouldn't like to admit the truth, often our independent spirit reduces God to either an interruption or an interpretation. Nevertheless, while we are dubious, the whole God business is kept around like a parachute in an airplane. We don't expect to use the equipment, but just in case . . .

Until some experience shakes us loose, we may not even be aware of our viewpoint. We are so preoccupied with ourselves we fail to realize how vast God's potential can be in our lives. Saint Augustine recognized what we miss. He observed God always wants to give us so much more but cannot because our hands are full and we have no place to receive the gifts.

Our all-sufficiency is frightening when the "all" excludes God. That's why Jesus considered the vices of the destitute far more leniently than He did the sins of the rich and successful. The prostitute and thief are never in danger of finding their present condition so satisfactory that God will never be a need. But the pride of the self-sufficient traps us into leaving God out.

Suddenly with the unexpected calamities, the blade falls! In the severing crunch of the metal cutting through to the chopping block, all illusions are clarified. The shattering thud crumples our self-delusions and exposes the emptiness of the preoccupations that have cluttered our minds. In the hour of disaster, we are more than anxious to discover if the parachute will open! But how much more important might be the discovery that God is far more than a mere rescuer of the floundering and the failing.

The Alternative: God Our Contemporary

Understanding and experiencing the loving care of God is much more valuable than simply receiving reprieve from Him. Knowing the Giver far surpasses whatever the Giver gives. So, when you enter into your own personal encounter with God you find not only the prime moving force in the universe but also the fundamental source that will make sense out of your total life. Reaching that point gives meaning and purpose to all that came before and will come after.

But let me share a word of warning. Suffering will not necessarily produce illumination. In fact, hardship may only deepen your conviction that you can depend only on yourself. Your loneliness can be deepened. You may even become certain there are no final answers. Multitudes have been shriveled and embittered by the same situations that brought others to sainthood.

You have to make the decision that just maybe God is out there hidden in the midst of misery. The Giver is found only as you release your reservations and walk open-armed into the mystery.

Paul had his own personal convictions about the results of this excursion: "We had the experience of coming to the end of our tether that we might learn to trust not in ourselves, but in God who can raise the dead" (2 Cor. 1:9, *Phillips*).

Through the times of insufficiency I am able to realize the utter sufficiency and capacity of the Father. Perhaps no life experience is more devastating than having to face our inadequacy. Yet by the same token, no other opportunity can lead us to the final answers that are only found at the end of our rope.

I can remember vividly the first time I saw the young mother so bent on suicide. Her face was contorted with pain. She conveyed a strange blend of anger and sheer desperation.

Why had she come to see me? A friend persuaded her, because death was so final. She owed it to herself to at least make a last effort to find hope. So, she came, doubting but open.

And her despair was well founded! For years she had struggled getting her husband through medical school. Even with several small children, the sacrifices had been worth the price. Janet loved Bob deeply. She hadn't considered any other life than one with him.

They had their problems but the marriage maintained a carefree abandonment. With medical school ending, a new fullness was just ahead. Then the axe fell for Janet.

Out of the clear blue, she uncovered Bob's involvement with a nurse. The liaison had confused Bob. He liked his wife's mind and the nurse's body. The result tore Janet's dreams and hopes into shreds.

As her problems poured out, the agony became greater. Bob was more than just a husband. He was Janet's god. Their relationship gave her life meaning and purpose. Janet's entire destiny had been wrapped up in the marriage. In addition to losing her husband, Janet was witnessing the death of her god.

Without hope or future, suicide seemed to be the only alternative. She was at the end of her tether.

After several sessions I interpreted what I felt was

86

happening. She quickly confirmed my diagnosis of a deteriorating god. We discussed what the real God might be like and the difference the discovery could make. Then Janet leveled with me.

"I can't believe in a God. Bob and I have been into science so deeply all these years we lost the ability to believe in anything beyond right now. I really want to accept what you are telling me as being true. But I just can't." Her voice broke and then her tone changed. She seemed distant and melancholy. "My last few years have been absorbed in accepting only what is provable. Oh, I wish I could believe what you're telling me!"

Desperation oozed through her tears. But her mind had been so filled with other ideas there just wasn't room for the truth. Even while planning the funeral of her corrupted god, she saw no possible resurrections on the horizon.

So I proposed an idea. "Look Janet, if you believe in investigation and proving truth, would you try an experiment to see if your arms might find Something else to embrace? Would you give yourself 30 days to find out if there is a God? Then if there's not, at the end of the month I'll jump off the building with you."

Her laughter at that thought broke the tension. But the pause also caused her to take the suggestion seriously. I described an experiment to learn how to talk to "Whatever" might be out or up there. Each day she was to take out 15 to 30 minutes to be absolutely alone. She must get away from phones, children, doorbells, and every interruption. Then in silence she was to envision "Someone" sitting across from her. I suggested she put a face on this figure. The face should be how she might envision Jesus of Nazareth looked. And she did have a mental picture of Him being a kind and understanding person who returned love for hate.

"Now, Janet. I want you to talk into that silence that is shaped like Jesus. Don't make up special phrases or worry about appropriate words. Just pour out every feeling you have. Take all of your anger and anxiety and tell Him about your worries. Get mad! Be sad! Be yourself! Lay every need on the table just as if someone *really* was there."

I suggested, as she released her flood of fear she might listen to hear if anything would come back within her. To be truly "scientific," she would have to experiment as if all of this was for real, believing that the whole experience is true. She agreed she would give it an honest try for the next 30 days.

She left. I settled back in my chair. Frankly, I was apprehensive! What if this "spur of the moment" idea was just something that had run through my head and God wasn't in it? After all, you can't make mistakes with people who are contemplating suicide! I decided to pray about this one at least twice a day!

Five days later Janet called. Timidly I asked, "Well, what's happening?"

"It's strange," she began. "This is the most unusual experience I've had in a long time. I'm beginning to get this eerie feeling that someone is in the room with me."

"Oh really!" I said, trying to be rather casual about the result. "Well, to be scientific you sure have to find out what's going on."

She agreed to keep trying. Now her compliance had a touch of enthusiasm.

In 10 days, Janet was back in my office sharing the wonder of her personal discovery. Yes, God was real. Yes, amazingly God was in that room with her. Oh yes, the Holy Spirit was moving in her life. And now the tears erupted from a spring of living water.

Though the divorce was inevitable, Janet had a new

God and a new source of joy. Her sadness remained, but now there was something to do with the hurt. Her growth in this new sufficiency jarred her friends. One even called to share with me the amazement of seeing a conversion actually happen. But I had to confess that I had nothing to do with the transaction!

In the quiet solitude of her room Janet had come to the end of her tether and gone beyond. Completely alone with God, the matter was settled. Like Paul she found that the Father had preserved her from imminent death. Indeed, now she could trust Him to keep her safe in the future.

I'm Christian, I'm Exempted

One other illusion needs to be considered. Many of us feel that any visitation of pain in our lives is simply an unfair management practice on God's part. Christians tend to carry an innate conviction that we should be exempted from the normal experiences of the human race. Our faith ought to be a guarantee against tragedy. After all, we are on a first-name basis with the Management!

Certainly the Bible teaches that our heavenly Father doesn't send harm. As Paul taught us, "He is the source of all mercy and comfort." However, most of us expect to avoid *any* of the problems that come with life on this planet because we are a part of Jesus' group.

That illusion not only sets us up for some real tumbles, but the deception keeps us from real usefulness to our Lord. When the mirage breaks, membership is then possible in the fellowship of Christ's suffering.

God has a unique method He has used through the centuries to convey the fullness of His love. The subtlety may elude us at first. But once we understand this operation the insight alone will change us.

Paul's concise statement was, "The more we share Christ's suffering, the more we are able to give of His encouragement." Did you notice the irony?

While we try to avoid conflict, Jesus Christ intentionally engaged hardship! Taking on hardship provided the clearest means of demonstrating God's love. In taking sin upon Himself, Jesus Christ uniquely used the only method that would heal the wounded world. Paul suggests that we can do the same in our own limited way. By sharing the burden of other people's lives, we will be able to manifest the love that redeems. Truly our greatest opportunity is to participate in Christ's suffering on behalf of humanity.

Granted, no promise of a rose garden is hidden behind the door! True, I find writing about Christ's suffering much easier than entering through the gate. But as any illusions about evading pain disappear, certainly I discover how to patiently encourage others to endure. In fact, I don't even have the right to use the word endurance until I've lived through times that teach me how hard it can be to just keep going! Later, after I have endured the problem with the help of Christ, my counsel will have a new ring of authenticity.

Only through suffering's opportunities can any of us gain the right to assure others that they too can find the real comfort and encouragement of God. Trite, glib words of pious hope that have never been tested irritate and incense anyone going through the fire. However, when we show our scars and reveal the bruise in our souls, then our prayer of encouragement truly becomes God speaking His word at that very moment.

Like steel that is made only in the hottest fire, so the other-centered, God-centered life arises only out of life's crucible of unrelenting conflict. Perhaps you feel the fierce heat would expose you to be only soft, spineless lead that will melt at the lowest temperature. Maybe, but I suspect after the slag has melted away, your life will be tempered so that you can support emotional weight that would break others.

The Alternative: Become Burden Bearers

Sorrow and sickness ultimately can soften and refine the personality. Tribulation and bereavement do not break the Christian but can produce a better person. Out of chaos, a new creation will arise to help all who come within the perimeter of that person's love.

For example, Elizabeth Barrett Browning saw her brother drown. The reaction of her sensitive nature was so severe that for years she was in emotional retreat. Later, when she married Robert Browning, her father violently rejected her. He refused to mention her name and left her out of his will. Once again the reverberations of affliction rattled in her soul.

Yet the furnace of misery shaped the mind and heart of one of the world's greatest poets. Her immortal verses were the result of every moment of that personal struggle. Unique words came out of her mourning that soothe the heart of every mourner.

The poem entitled "Substitution" is her personal confirmation of the same conviction that Paul carried about the encouragement born in our distress.

> When some beloved voice that was to you
> Both sound and sweetness, faileth suddenly,
> And silence, against which you dare not cry
> Aches round you like a strong disease and
>   new—
> What hope? What help? What music will
>   undo
> That silence to your sense?

Not friendship's sight,
Not reason's subtle count; not melody
Of viols, nor of pipes that Faunus blew;
Not songs of poets, nor nightingales
Whose hearts leap upward
    through the cypress trees
To the clear moon; nor yet the spheric laws
Self-chanted, nor the angels sweet "All hails,"
Met in the smile of God: nay, none of these.
Speak Thou, availing Christ!—and fill this
pause.[2]

Indeed, to participate in Christ's suffering is to learn to help others find a substitute for the deathly quiet pauses that fall in their lives. Without this visitation of pain our words stay forever hollow.

Those who become burden bearers always profit from what they can't escape. The following testimony, attributed to an unknown Confederate soldier, guides my supplications and puts perspective back into life as I repeat it:

I asked for strength that I might achieve;
    He made me weak that I might obey.
I asked for health
that I might do greater things.
    I was given grace
    that I might do better things.
I asked for riches that I might be happy;
    I was given poverty that I might be wise.
I asked for power
that I might have the praise of men;
    I was given weakness
    that I might feel the need of God.
I asked for all things that I might enjoy life;

I was given life that I might enjoy all things.
I received nothing that I asked for,
 all that I hoped for,
     My prayer was answered.[3]

Thank you Lord, for every minute of my life. Amen.

Some Concluding Thoughts

Where is the Holy Spirit at work today? One conclusion is absolutely certain. He ministers wherever people hurt. By entering into the needs of others, I have the opportunity of sharing the presence of Christ. All I need is the sensitivity to recognize where the hurting of mankind and the redemptive work of Christ intersect. The Christ is always found on that cross.

Because renewed sensitivity reveals that conclusion, pain is profitable. My inner eyes are opened and my ears hear the hidden cries of others. As long as I am isolated in comfort and insensitive in my caring, I will never recognize Jesus as He comes by in "the least of these." But when my illusions are stripped away the true human condition is revealed. So suffering is very valuable.

Indeed, all of these poor needy friends of Jesus are your brothers too. Again, the cost is quite worthwhile if your aches and pains bring you closer to others. Perhaps, the heavenly Father is withholding a startling miracle right now because in His plan you are to be someone's answer. Is it possible He wants you to be His miracle today? Just this thought alone is reparation for many a discouraging hour.

Some Questions to Ponder

1. What have you learned from your painful experiences? Have you become more sensitive to others' needs?

93

2. Do you recognize "broken people" around you who hide behind "an appearance of well-being," but who need help? What can you do to help bring wholeness to someone like that today?
3. Maybe you are the one who is hiding behind a mask. How are you trying to "fight the dragons" alone? In what area of your life or in what relationship are you trapped by self-sufficiency to the extent that you have left God out of your life? What are you going to do about this condition right now? Do you know someone who can share this burden with you?
4. Do you believe that Christians try to avoid hardship and suffering? Does Christ promise to protect us from trials?

Notes

1. Catherine Marshall, *Beyond Ourselves* (New York: McGraw-Hill Book Co., 1961), p. 149.
2. Elizabeth Barrett Browning, "Substitution," *Masterpieces of Religious Verse*, ed. James Dalton Morrison (New York: Harper and Row Publishers, Inc., 1948), p. 201.
3. Garth and Merv Rosell, comp., *"Shoe-Leather" Faith* (St. Paul: Bruce Publishing, 1960), Selection No. 212.

five

A Personal Conversation with Jesus

Jesus had just finished teaching about eternal life. He talked of heavenly mansions of many rooms. In my usual thoughtless way I blurted out, "And you came just so I could go to heaven!"

Jesus looked appalled. Apparently I had missed the real point. "I didn't come so you could 'go to heaven.' What a self-indulgent twist you give my teaching."

Obviously I had badly misunderstood. I protested, "But Lord, I thought you said—"

"Once again you listened with the ears of indulgence. You avoid pain even if it is profitable. You seek comfort even when it robs you of growth. And now you would turn my words into nothing more than a guarantee of eternal existence."

I thought to myself that heaven surely was the point of His coming. "There is something *more* than heaven?"

"I came that you might have a relationship with the Father. My talk of eternity was to give you the assurance of an unbroken and unending relationship with the Father. I spoke that you would know that nothing can separate you from Him, not even death. But your goal is not to be heaven; rather it is to seek your relationship with the Father.

"Don't worry about the world around you and don't be concerned with the world above you. But let everything water and nourish your knowledge of the Father."

The Power in PAIN

As I remember, the phone rang around 2:00 in the morning. Fumbling for the receiver I wasn't even sure that the noise wasn't a bad dream. The call proved to be much more than only a nightmare.

Her voice was trembling. Though I was barely awake the tone didn't conceal the avalanche of emotion waiting to break past each word. "Robert, I'm sorry to be calling so late but I didn't know who else to phone. I just have to talk to someone! I can't stand sitting here in the dark right now."

Without any idea of what was going on, I assured Alice the call was O.K. Rubbing my eyes, I sat up on my pillow expecting to hear some routine family problem thrust upon my needed rest.

With surprisingly steady calm she unleashed the explosion in one sentence. "George just shot himself in the head!" There was a pause that seemed to last an eternity. From then on her feelings rushed out.

Their problems began the day they stepped over the threshold. Unknown to Alice, George had fought a life-long battle with depression. He held things inside until the least difficulty mushroomed beyond any justifiable proportion. Finally, he would sink into a discussion of suicide as the only way out. She had tried to find outside help but he wouldn't see a counselor. Ultimately, divorce seemed the only way she could keep her sanity.

On this evening he had knocked on the door. When she answered he began saying incoherent and disconnected sentences. Quite suddenly out of nowhere the gun appeared. Before her terrified eyes, he shot himself in the head.

As he crumpled, much more than could be seen fell to the ground. Faith, hope, forebearance seemed to flow together into a puddle of uselessness. Is there any consolation for such a dark, empty night?

Much later, Alice and I sat down to sort out the meaning of that night and to try and find direction for the rest of her life. This chapter contains some of the insights I shared with her. She found these ideas helped her get in touch with the power of God. Eventually Alice found renewed hope and sustenance for her life. She pushed on until she gained the strength of the Holy Spirit. So with her, let's dig deeper to find the power that is available to help us in our pain.

Is God with Us or Against Us?

When the night is troubled by confusion and crying, we must know whether God is for or against us. When the sky breaks into pieces that fall at our feet, we need assurance that the heavenly Father's wish is for us to find His strength to sustain our night of difficulty. He does not want us to hurt. Alice had to know if God stood with her.

What can we learn from Jesus? A characteristic of Jesus' ministry was His sensitivity to whatever besieged the human heart. Day and night He labored to ease the bent back and lighten the heavy heart. As the total embodiment of the Father's will, Jesus attacked the network center of grief and malice.

Jesus taught that He was the fulfillment of Isaiah's vision of hope for the suffering. Jesus took upon Himself the releasing of the captives, the recovering of sight to the blind, the freeing of the oppressed (see Isa. 42:6,7). During the whole of His ministry, Jesus demonstrated that God stands with the dispossessed. When hurting happens, God is present. If God sent pain intentionally why would Jesus have spent His whole ministry healing man? He would have been at complete odds with His Father.

So, you hurt? Do you feel as though you've been victimized and oppressed by fate? Has a blindness dropped over your sense of direction? Remember, Jesus' works demonstrated that God resides with the humble and the broken. Though your emotions ache and throb, God is, indeed, very much with you right now. Consider your pain to be a confirmation of His caring.

No, He is not against you. What you can't see is not the measure of what is there. Remember, despair is only an index to your need. Emptiness is not a gauge of God's concern. Rather, Jesus put flesh to the promise that God abides with the broken and bent.

So we can always start with the confidence that God stands against suffering. Regardless of what has happened, we should know that our heavenly Father is working on our behalf to remove the thorns from the path. His eyes are never closed to our afflictions.

But Don't Ask Why

Once we feel that God is on our side, universally we seem to have an initial question for Him. Our probing minds always seize on a particular issue. Why has this happened to us? The basic human hunger for meaning must find a purpose for our tragedies.

Why has this happened to me? Or the inflection may be, "Why has this happened to *me?*" Regardless of the emphasis, the lack of an answer may lead us to even deeper despair. In fact, as I shared in the introduction, this book began to happen out of my own frantic need to find an explanation for suffering that had become personal to me.

And I have come to a conclusion about this question. Knowing that God stands with me means that I really don't have to have an answer for the all-mysterious "whys" of my life. In fact, that question generally leads nowhere but to confusion.

There are never fully satisfying reasons. In a world of cleft palates, flaming gas truck collisions with passenger cars, and cancer attacks, the causes can be hopelessly complex. Often people are careless or indifferent. Sometimes prenatal care was inadequate. Human irresponsibility does abound! But searching through the "whys" never brings a settling peace to your heart.

So, I've quit asking *why* do tragedies occur. That question has been traded in for a better one. Now I seek to know *what* can this mean. How can God use my calamity? When the curtain drops, I don't pray to understand the reason. Looking back to "why" is of no value.

Rather I point my face forward and start a whole new conversation. "O.K. God, here we go. I don't know where but I do believe you will re-weave the tear into a better design. So I'll trust you for tomorrow." Exchanging "why" for "what" will put power in your path!

My clue came a long time before I realized what I had discovered. During my college years I majored in humanities and read the great Russian writers at length. A theme that kept surfacing intrigued me. This reshaping of *why* into *what* was one of the undercurrents of the great Christian novelists like Tolstoy and Dostoevski.

Particularly intriguing was Feodor Dostoevski's insights in his book *The Brothers Karamazov.* Later I discovered that his profound insights were a by-product of what formed his writing. Because of his social protest against the cruelty of the Czar he was sentenced to a slave camp in Siberia. As the cattle-car prisoner train was pulling away, a peasant woman thrust a copy of the New Testament into Feodor's hand. Though he was an atheist, the little Bible was his only link with the outside world for the next terror-filled years.

With no alternative, Dostoevski began to read and re-read those pages. Around him men were dying of cold and disease. As the cruelty and terror increased, so did his grasp of the meaning of those words on each tiny page. In time, he came to nearly memorize the whole of the New Testament.

There could never be valid reasons for the vile inhuman waste of life Dostoevski experienced. But the power of God to transcend evil and heal human wounds started to rise like the sun over the frozen Siberian horizon. Spiritual scales fell from his unbelieving eyes and a new vision of God formed in the frustrated mind of a deeply caring man. From the barrenness of the tundra arose the fruitful abundance of those great novels. Dostoevski found God had turned his whys into powerful whats.

Mystery always surrounds life. No single question

can penetrate to the center and seldom can one answer be all-inclusive. But our Father's benevolence bubbles up from the center and He brings fall's better harvest. Frustration and anxiety give way to patience and waiting. Our railing and ranting is turned into thoughtfulness and reflective anticipation.

In her contact with modern Russians, Suzanne Massie found that they still have this same consolation Dostoevski discovered. While she and her husband were doing research in Russia for Robert Massie's widely acclaimed *Nicholas and Alexandra*, Suzanne had opportunity to touch this same strand that still runs through the Russian soul.

Much hardship and adversity has long since stripped the Soviet Christians of wondering about satisfying reasons. But what strength they have found for their unpretentious encounter with life! The Massies had their own struggle with a hemophiliac son who constantly stood on the brink of death. While Suzanne was battling her own fears about this boy's life, a Russian poet sent her his encouragement:

> Perhaps we are all only witnesses in a single
> enormous trial whose outcome is unclear, but
> certain. We can only occasionally perceive its
> outline as when behind a driving rain, we can
> sometimes glimpse the silhouettes of angels.[1]

When the rains come again we can all watch into the night. This time the shape in the cold does not have to be the old enemy Mr. Why. Someone much more redemptive waits for us in every dark night.

Not a Puzzle but a Mystery
Recently I stumbled across a quote I've been unable

to trace. "Life is not a puzzle to be solved. It is a mystery to be lived." Perhaps a Russian Christian wrote that. At least the author understood God is not a Divine computer. His very Being of love is bathed in marvelous mystery. So, we come closer to His power, not by insight as much as by trusting that He supports all of life. The unknown is not to be feared.

How often have we tried to turn the will of God into a mathematical formula that brings certain results! Evangelicals are perhaps the worst at trying to prove what God actually intends. They want infallible reasons for their decisions. For a period of my life I had several marvelous talks on how to know exactly what God purposes. If you followed my simple procedures you could know everything with all of life's guesses removed!

How silly this was! While faith can know clear direction and our heavenly Father certainly can show us exactly what He has planned, do we think we can reduce His mind to some ecclesiastical slide rule? No, the mystery is so much more intricate than any puzzle.

Actually we want perfect solutions so we won't have to bear the awesome pain of thinking and deciding. Oh yes, coming to full maturity is heady business. But, we prefer the infant status where God gets all the credit or blame for what befalls.

Real life is different. God's planning defies simplistic explorations. His will is an "always going forward" kind of concern. But there are always pluses and minuses. Jesus didn't promise a primrose path but only that we would never stop going onward.

For example, we prayed about going to seminary. Just the right place was crucial. We knew we were being directed to His perfect place for my education. However, shortly after my studies began I was deeply disappointed. Rather than a place of nurture where I could sit back and absorb truth, this school was a theological battleground. Professors were not friends trying to build my faith, they were adversaries seemingly trapped in their own doubts. Surely this was not God's will! What a mistake!

Yet, at that place and time, I received critical experiences that clarify the chuckholes in today's road. The negative environment built a faith filled with campaign-tested insights tried by the sword. Though I now know the seminary had a very poor and inadequate philosophy of education, God used even the minuses.

Paul reflected on these mysteries: "I consider that the sufferings of this present time are not worthy to be compared with the glory that is to be revealed to us" (Rom. 8:18). I think he had two things in mind as he pointed forward. Certainly the glory of eternity will make the struggles of the present age unmentionable. But in addition, in our living, we will come to see out of our own experiences the brighter light of God's power at work.

That certainty of eternity in the now is expressed in a letter that Mike Yaconelli wrote to a congregation that had called him to the ministry of their church. Mike is nationally known as a clever, witty youth specialist. You don't expect razzle-dazzle youth pastors to have any *real* problems. So the jolt was double when he explained he couldn't come because of his two-year-old daughter's condition. Mike's letter said:

> As all know by now, it has been about two months since we discovered that our two-year-old daughter, Lisa, has cancer. Of course, things aren't back to normal—they never will be. For the time being, God's wish for us to travel, to be with you has been sty-

mied, stopped. But God has not stopped—His will will be accomplished ultimately. Evil has won for the moment and the pain inflicted by its victory is not less painful because we know that God, even in this, can use it for our good. Once Joe Bayley (who has had three of his children die of separate diseases) said to us, "Don't doubt in the darkness what God has shown you in the light." We haven't! Someday we will be coming to you folks, but for now we will live a day at a time, knowing that God is there, knowing that He has a will for us where we are, and knowing that someday we will be able to ask God some very hard questions.

Eternity does change our considerations. Truly there is power in knowing that ultimately our questions will be turned into affirmations. We can even enjoy living through the mystery without having to stumble over the pieces in the puzzle.

Order Out of Chaos

Here's another insight to help carry you through the difficult times. Our heavenly Father is the God of order. He is constantly at work bringing direction out of chaos. The first words of Genesis tell us that the world began when God brought shape out of void (see Gen. 1:1,2). And He is still concerned to accomplish the same result in each of our lives.

Chaos is deceptive. We too quickly write off confusion as having no possibility of direction. In the seeming aimlessness of disorder the world appears to move without principle or design. Those who embrace this belief are only a breath away from despair.

The IBM Company produced an amazing machine that demonstrates that even chaos cannot escape being ordered by a purposeful universe. Their strange machine keeps hurling large quantities of small balls through the air. As you watch, a principle begins to emerge. Regardless of how the little balls are hurled, they finally fall into a regular pattern. What an astounding law of physics is working! The greater the chaos, the greater will be the final order. Behind the derangement is complete arrangement. Thus, the world of physics displays one dimension of the way in which God always stands at the center.

So, your disorder is only the prelude to the discovery of hidden purpose. The sovereignty of God guarantees that every event will find a place in the larger scheme of things. And your personal dilemmas are all a part of this plan.

During a trip to the Middle East I found the same principle at work in the secret of oriental rugs. Each magnificent tapestry is produced by the most unusual method. Threads and twine are stretched across large wooden frames that may reach to the ceiling The artisan stands on one side of the loom. Boys with threads stand on the back side. Neither knows what appears on the front side. As production begins the artist starts shouting instructions for the thread to come through.

Swiftly and directly the work begins to take shape. But unavoidably the threads do not follow the master weaver's direction. Wrong colors or twisted direction in the pattern is inevitable. In fact, these irregularities are the mark of a genuine Persian carpet.

However, the sign of the great rug maker is his ability to take any mistake and re-weave it back into the total pattern. As the design continues, the flaw becomes an asset. The careful eye will detect that the twist was not

105

the master's intention. Yet, the mistake has been swept away in a new blend of brilliant red or yellow. No longer is the error an object of disdain.

Sooner or later, every one of us will find the fabric of our lives torn and violently ripped. As the frayed edges stand exposed our whole being may feel naked and annihilated. Nevertheless, we can rest with a newfound confidence. The Master Weaver will not only mend the tear but He will re-weave the fabric into an even more meaningful design. What He did not will, He uses anyway.

Is God, in this present moment, reordering, re-weaving lives? How does the Master Weaver's skill make a difference when the actual circumstances of hardship have not changed? In what ways does the eternal principle of order apply to our lives today? Well, consider the story of Neal Jeffrey.

Ron Davis, a Presbyterian minister in Minnesota, became acquainted with this shy, quiet, young man during his work with the Fellowship of Christian Athletes. Ron was a worker on the college staff and Neal was still just a high school kid. As their relationship deepened, Ron discovered why this handsome athlete was so quiet. He was afflicted with a chronic speech impediment. Neal could not say anything without breaking into painful stammering that turned every sentence into a comedy routine.

The problem took an even more ironic twist. Neal's father is one of the finest inspirational speakers in America. James Jeffrey is the president of the Fellowship of Christian Athletes. In this role he has spoken to thousands of young people with deeply stirring messages. The father uses words to change lives and the son couldn't even speak two words and get them to come out right!

Because of Neal's deep, personal spirituality Ron wanted to keep in touch. He wondered how God could ever work through such a sad affliction. The boy loved God and still the problem persisted. But in time Ron lost track of Neal.

Suddenly the sports pages came to life with the story of Baylor winning their first conference football championship in 50 years. Their unusual quarterback had to stutter the signals to his teammates. At the season's end Neal Jeffrey was named the outstanding player in the Southwest Conference.

That summer Ron found Neal at an FCA conference. Amazingly, Neal was to speak that evening to over a thousand boys. Ron waited for some miracle to usher forth coherent sounds forming beautiful words.

But no miracle of tongues appeared. As Neal began to unfold his testimony the audience broke into laughter. Surely this was an evening skit. Nobody talks like that in front of a large audience except a comedian. Slowly and painfully the audience realized the laughter was just one more cruel response to a young athlete's attempts to communicate.

He must have talked for 30 minutes. Anyone else could have delivered the talk in maybe 10 or 15 minutes. Yet, something very special started to happen. Neal talked about a God who loved him just as he was. With his inadequacies, God's love came in a personal way. As the silence deepened, he shared that God doesn't always remove the hard times. Even better, our heavenly Father moves us through the difficult places with a power that strengthens us for all of our life's other needs. So Neal opened his heart to reveal how God had not removed this speech impediment but through his weakness God gave him strength. At the end of the half hour, he stammered out a call for commitments to Jesus

Christ. He didn't promise an easy way out but plenty of strength for the journey.

The FCA staff was staggered by the response. Never before in any such meeting had so many young people moved forward to give their lives to Jesus Christ. Of all the beautiful speeches, none had the miraculous effects of the twisted words of Neal Jeffrey.

And our heavenly Father is just as concerned to use your needs as His opportunity. Even the momentary confusion of problems cannot keep Him from bringing order into your life again.

So Don't Run Away!

Perhaps, the most natural reaction to tragedy is to want to run. If there was a rock big enough or a hole deep enough, we'd just disappear. It is natural to want to hide from people and to find yourself avoiding friends and old acquaintances.

Yet all of the reassurances we have discovered so far guarantee we don't have to become escapists. We do not have to acquiesce and retreat. Rather than evading issues, we can dare to face every situation head-on.

The ministry of the apostle Paul was one continuing example of fearlessly pressing on in the face of adversity. He once wrote: "What are you doing, weeping and breaking my heart? For I am ready not only to be bound but even to die at Jerusalem for the name of the Lord Jesus" (Acts 21:13). Even in the face of death, he didn't ask to avoid the cost or understand the necessity.

He was excited to be a part of the adventure.

This very passage carries the same promise for a modern Russian Christian. Alexander Solzhenitsyn wove its message into his monumental novel, *One Day in the Life of Ivan Denisovich*. After laboriously taking us through a day in a Stalinist work camp in Siberia, Solzhenitsyn brings us to the unavoidable question of what such an existence can mean.

The dialogue unfolds between the Christian Alyoshka and the hostile, caustic Ivan. Ivan doubts the value of religion unless praying can help escape their hellhole existence. Alyoshka explains that escape is unthinkable. Praying to have evil removed from one's heart is the more important thing. He implies the powerful answer is that the transformed man will change the place where he lives right now. He is completely ready to endure the cost of the prison for Christ's sake. And he quotes Acts 21:13. Even the terror of prison is full of meaning when Christ is in the cell with you.

From the worst of twentieth-century life, Solzhenitsyn has found his way to Christ. There is no asking for escape. He doesn't ask for all the answers. It is sufficient to proclaim the Christ who changes the malice in our hearts by using even the evil of the world as His tool. Indeed, this is meat for the journey.

And how can you make all of this power yours right now? What can you do to make sure your situation really is used by God? Once during an afternoon chat, I asked Corrie ten Boom to share some very practical suggestions with me from her own prison camp days. Her counsel has helped me understand the problems that don't seem to change.

Corrie and I are both members of the Reformed Church. We have a heritage that teaches us to have certain trust in the sovereignty of God. This deeply ingrained faith empowered Corrie to live through the terrible days of the Nazi concentration camps.

She suggested that I sit down with a pencil and paper and put my troubled questions and doubts down in black and white. Just writing out my hardest problems was very clarifying. Then, staring these dilemmas in the face,

I begin to pray over each doubt. But rather than asking for a change, Corrie suggested I transfer these concerns into the care of God. I should tell God I can't understand now what will happen then. But I am going to trust God for whatever the future brings. While I am unable to grasp reasons I will be confident that my letting go will allow Him to fully gain control. Finally I put a date on the paper.

Whenever I feel the fears and anxieties creeping back, I get out this piece of paper and remember my transaction. Then I just pray a prayer of further relinquishment.

On the back of the paper I keep a record of what I discover God is doing with these areas of need. With every new solution to a mystery I record what He is showing me. With the passing of time, my prayers of feeble release have grown into prayers of excited exclamation. Corrie was so right! When God holds the future, the results will always be glorious!

Many of her spiritual insights were shared with the world in *The Hiding Place*. There are no *whys* for Corrie because her life is too filled with the unfolding drama of the difference the *whats* are making.

God's power can transform our yesterdays too. "This is what the past is for! Every experience God gives us, every person He puts in our lives, is the perfect preparation for the future that only He can see."[2]

Some Concluding Thoughts

Two major pitfalls beckon us when disaster strikes. The first snare is to agonize over *why* the event has happened. While we can discover the general principles for how God operates in our world, it seems that answers for our personal calamities are usually elusive and unsatisfying. The inquiry is just frustrating. The second trap is acquiescence to defeat. Failure causes us to throw up our hands and retreat. By hiding and withdrawing, we admit evil has won. Should we ever concede defeat?

Never! The very nature of God stands against any such conclusion. The whole ministry of Jesus was an assurance that God's primary intention is always to heal pain. From the foundations of creation, God has always been at work to bring order out of chaos. Even our helplessness contains power when it is yielded up to the Father's intentions. Through the mysteriousness of life, He is at work bringing order to confusion and strength to weakness.

So learn to commit every dilemma into the concerned hands of your heavenly Father. While He expects you to continue to do everything possible, leave the worrying to God. His power will ultimately rebuild and redesign your life plan. God isn't ever defeated and you needn't be either.

Some Questions to Ponder

1. Does the statement in this chapter, "Consider your pain to be a confirmation of His caring," mean that God sends pain deliberately to show He cares for you? Read Isaiah 42:6,7 and the section "Is God with Us or Against Us?" in this chapter.

2. When pain and trouble strike you, and you are tempted to ask God "why," what should you really be looking for? What steps can you take to change your why questions into practical opportunities for God to work in your life?

3. Do you find yourself preoccupied with lots of "whys"? What steps can you take to change those questions into practical opportunities for God to work in your life?

4. Corrie ten Boom said, "Every person He puts in our lives is the perfect preparation for the future that only

He can see." Think of the key people in your life today and see if you can find why God has given them to you.

Notes

1. Robert and Suzanne Massie, *Journey* (New York: Alfred A. Knopf, Inc., 1975), p. 218.
2. Corrie ten Boom, *The Hiding Place* (Old Tappan, N.J.: Chosen Books, 1971), p. 6.

=====six=====

"Jesus, where does evil come from? Where does malice start?"

But He answered with a question. He asked me where I thought the source might be.

"Well, it seems that the heart of man is a likely place to look. Perhaps, people just haven't seen the good that I have found in you. Maybe we just haven't educated men well enough. When the right example is seen, then evil might disappear."

Jesus looked down and scratched in the dirt with His foot. Then His head came back and He spoke right up to the center of the sky.

"O Father, were that this were so! Then Our task would be easy and quick."

And He rubbed His palm as if some internal pain were yet to break through the skin.

113

Who's
to
BLAME?

The jaundice was still faintly evident in his face. Obviously he had a liver problem.

On the phone his wife had cautioned me that Nick was extremely nervous and upset. She said he paced endlessly in a state of utter despair. And it was true. In fact, he greeted me at the door with almost open hostility. I seemed to be a symbol of the cause of his black depression.

Just 24 hours before, Nick had gotten the straightforward verdict—he had cancer of the liver. Not only was it terminal, but at best he had three months left. The doctor gave the diagnosis and issued the death warrant in the same stroke.

Nick was a Russian immigrant who carried within him all the native, open, brutal honesty of his old culture. What he felt was what he said, loud and clear. He was mad, furious, distraught and ready to heap revenge somewhere, somehow, on someone for this visitation of tragedy.

"I'm going to die! Do you understand that? I am going to die and they are going to put me in the ground. They are going to throw dirt on my face. Do you understand that? I'm dying right now!"

I nodded. My mind was racing to find something to say, but nothing seemed better than just letting the silence work.

"You're supposed to know about God. You're supposed to talk to God. Well, why has this God decided to do this to me? Why have I been picked to just get blown away? What have I done that was so bad that He should reach out to put an end to my life?"

I mustered up a timid counseling response: "You seem to feel God has done this to you?"

"Seem to feel? Seem to feel? Of course I do! Who else did this to me? If there's a God, I want to know why He's done this terrible thing to me, to my wife, to my family!"

And then he broke down into sobs of anguish.

Nick's plea of "why me," is representative of all humanity. In his despair, he felt that the source of his condition must be established. If he had been arbitrarily picked to go to the bone pile, then any words of pious comfort would be just sore lies. Unless he could see a satisfactory reason for his condition, there could be no comfort for him as he faced death.

That scene has been enacted a billion times. When our life is unexpectedly shortened, when our potential is wiped out, when our mate is left to face lonely days, we want an answer. Who is to blame for this? Who has done this to me?

115

Sometimes we may say "who" and sometimes "what." But it all amounts to the same thing. We all feel urged to make sense out of our tragedy. Desperately, we hunt a way to put in order the disorder that has descended into our lives.

Nick's problem was in believing that God was really trustworthy. He wanted assurance that God is the Father and not *Der Fuehrer!* Is God completely benevolent? Or is there a possibility that He intentionally does bad things to us? Nick's fear and anger were justified. He was talking about *his* death.

Well, what would you say to my friend Nick? How would you answer his anxieties? Why not lay the book down and think about it just a minute before you go on.

What did you come up with?

Perhaps, you thought about what we said in the preceding chapters—how paradoxical pain can be, or how God uses for His redemptive purposes even that which He doesn't intend. To talk about how pain can be reclaimed could be of value. Or discussing the profit that can develop out of calamity might be a good response.

And with these answers you would be reassuring Nick that while a miracle hadn't happened, God was still at work for him. But Nick's brilliant and honest mind wouldn't let you off the hook that easy. He would still want to know where his problem came from.

Nicks' problem is an area we haven't actually covered. In the other chapters we have aimed at leading the suffering person out of the maze of emotional confusion that comes with tragedy. So what can we say to the most basic question of all? What is the origin of evil and suffering?

Let us offer three explanations we often hear for the source of adversity. Let's see if they could satisfy a man who is facing death within three months.

Possible Pacifiers for Pain

First, we are told that we live in a "fallen world," a very imperfect planet. Because the world has flaws, we inevitably get caught with problems that are not our fault.

In chapter 3 we analyzed why God would allow these inconsistencies to exist. The conclusion is that the dilemmas are not bad because they allow greater things to happen. There is a price to be paid for the good things that are always before us.

O.K., I find those insights help a great deal, but they are not a satisfactory answer to the questions Nick was asking. I found the "fallen world" theory an incomplete answer several years before when I visited Arlington National Cemetery. The first impression of that place has haunted me many times.

The hour was quite early, just at the time the huge bronze gates swung open. Cold winter fog and snow clung to every tree and grave marker.

I was totally unprepared for the sight of row on row on row of silent, uniform, sterile, white grave markers, perfectly in line and precisely diagonal, as far as the eye could see. This final perfect ordering of death made the horror of war's disorder even more stark. Here covered with grass and marble, are the mementos of a nation's most difficult hours.

With me was a young woman whose father was buried on the side of one of these hills. He had been a distinguished chaplain. In a quiet unhurried way, we found our path to his grave. She knelt and brushed snow away from the container to place her small handful of flowers on her father's final resting place. Like the silence of this park, tears began to cover her face.

As I surveyed the hills standing in memorial to the carnage of war, Nick's question was already there. Did Someone cause this? Who can we blame for the endless

117

tears that have been shed in this place? Who is responsible for the Arlington Cemeteries of our world?

Just saying that our world is "fallen" is not enough; there has to be a more adequate answer.

A second answer is that such evil is the result of the weakness of mankind. Because of our limitations as human beings we get anxious. That anxiety causes us to do all kinds of self-centered things to protect ourselves. The result is that we are constantly harming the rest of the human race in our selfish attempts to make ourselves secure. So wars and murder arise out of the corrupted heart of mankind.

That explanation has led to the idea that evil is merely the absence of good. If we can just get enough positive input into the human race, there will be no more Arlington Cemeteries. So our answer to evil is found in modern education! When people have been adequately informed they will naturally make the right decisions.

Though this secular answer is the most prevalent explanation for evil, it is the most naive of all. Sober reflection on World War II and what has followed exposes the shallowness of that proposition.

All of the evil and terror of Nazi Germany did not arise out of ignorance or lack of culture. Germany was one of the most literate countries in the world with the highest level of learning and scientific achievement. Yet, men with Ph.D.'s perfected the death camps. Informed people voted for Hitler. Men of science used Jews for inhuman experiments. There was no lack of education in the Third Reich but, at the same time, there was no limit to the horrors.

The modern explanation for evil becomes even more shaky as we consider more recent history. The atom bomb era wasn't the product of superstition. Technology at the highest level seems only to compound our ability to destroy ourselves! No, modern education hasn't been the answer to evil at all.

And of course, that rationale doesn't help Nick with his cancer condition.

The third and most common answer is that whatever has happened is God's will. While we hedge at saying catastrophes like Hitler and the Jewish holocaust are God's will, we assure each other that our personal tragedies are in some way still His intentions.

We say that God wants it all to happen. By divine design and forethought the pieces of the puzzle are arranged to come together in the final tragedy over which we grieve. These words of counsel are supposed to reassure us. When we accept this explanation, it makes everything O.K. God designed the disaster, so now we should feel good about it all. This is the standard easy answer. God gets all the credit or blame.

Frankly, I have never been able to stomach that explanation. Moreover, the general use of "God's will" as the last catch-all makes me angry. Should that response be true, I, along with Nick, would have to be mad at God. Since I can't accept the phrase as all inclusive, I get very uneasy with people who trivialize God's will. Their effect is to pat us on the head, kiss our hurt finger, and send us back to play outdoors once again.

"Smile, it's God's will."

God's will becomes a drape to throw over problems we don't want to explore. The divine shroud is dropped over the issue to stifle and avoid any in-depth encounter with the hard side of life. General usage implies, "Don't think, just accept."

Don't misunderstand me. I do have great respect for the mystery that always remains at the center of life. There is a great cloud of unknowing that cannot be rationally penetrated. Our faith in God does help to give handles for what we could never encompass with our minds.

Here's my point. There is a difference between mystery and ignorance. Mystery is what remains after my deepest inquiry has been exhausted. But ignorance refuses to even explore. It is a cover for cowardice that will not venture forth into the mystery. "Don't think. Just accept."

I have already warned you that if you want to take this route I won't walk with you. Dishonesty, particularly in God's name, is a dead-end street. Any explanation that won't stand up to honest and thorough examination isn't worth holding.

I find an even more difficult problem: If all the terror is God's will, then what kind of God do we have? I believe this dilemma is what has turned men like Albert Camus into atheists. The father of modern existential doubt didn't just happen into his deep despair and pessimism. Out of the hardness of his experience, Camus came to the verdict that life is absurd. His final conclusion was that living made him nauseated.

Why such bitterness? Because as he fought in the French underground during World War II, he saw unspeakable horror. His adventures forced him to a single conclusion. If God stood behind this, then He is indeed even more terrible than men. The other possibility was that there really must not be a God at all! On the basis of either premise, he concluded life has no meaning.

What loneliness must have lived in this man's soul! When you read his novels you want to cry at his being caught in such an empty, void world. But Camus isn't alone. He is just more honest than many would dare to be.

There are thousands of depressed people who mutter in despair, "I guess it was God's will." Really they are afraid to say any more. But deep in their unconscious recesses an inner horror wants to scream, "It isn't fair. It isn't right. Either God is evil or there is no God."

I remember watching that realization fall like a shroud on a tiny little mother from the Azores. Thousands of miles from home, the cold hand of tragedy knocked on her door. Her beautiful little baby daughter died. One of those strange medically unexplainable crib deaths visited her bassinet. Silence settled in her empty nursery and Maria wanted to know why.

As an answer, her father sent a poem to relieve her grief. The poem suggested that children are beautiful flowers given to adorn the creation and decorate the table of God. In this instance God went through creation and decided to take a small little rose for his enjoyment.

"God picks bouquets. This time he picked a little flower." Such was the father's counsel. The result was that Maria blindly accepted the explanation and lived in terror that God might come again for her next child.

No! Such a simple answer as "it is God's will" concludes many things that are far from simple. The implication is that God is insensitive, unconcerned, and maybe even monstrous in His actions.

Smile? It's God's will? We have to think the matter through again. This solution just doesn't add up with what I find when I read the Bible. Both the Old and the New Testaments give a very different picture of what God is like. Turn to the book of Psalms and look for themes that run through a great many of the individual passages. Consider:

> I waited patiently for the Lord; and He inclined to me, and heard my cry. He brought me up out of the pit of destruction, out of the

miry clay; and He set my feet upon a rock . . .
And he put a new song in my mouth, a song
of praise to our God (Ps. 40:1-3).

That certainly gives a very different picture of the way that God's will operates. Psalm 46 begins, "God is our refuge and strength, a very present help in trouble." Everywhere the note of affirmation leaps out at you! The phrase, "The steadfast love of the Lord endures forever," is found throughout the Old Testament. God's character is described with words like concern and caring, not capriciousness and callousness.

In the New Testament these abstract qualities take flesh in Jesus Christ. His whole ministry was spent binding up the brokenhearted. Again, we are given a picture of God and His will that doesn't square with Him as the source of tragedy. The accumulated wisdom and inspiration of the centuries find its highest expression in a simple sentence, "God is love" (1 John 4:8). The very essence of God's motivation and personhood is love and concern.

Obviously, there is a vast contradiction between the description of God in Scripture and what is popularly attributed to Him. So I find it impossible to blame tragedy on God.

This came back to me when I visited the Anne Frank house in Amsterdam. Years before, *The Diary of Anne Frank* had deeply touched me. And then seeing the movie version seared the story into my emotions. So when I went to Amsterdam the question returned, could God have been the cause of this little Jewish girl and her family being sent to their deaths?

Just as the escaping Jews had done, I entered the secret stairway concealed behind the bookcase-door. Those hidden stairs seemed so like the ones that led up to my daughter's bedroom at home. When I reached the attic I went straight for the room in which Anne had slept. There, still hung on the walls, are the pictures of her childhood heroines. The mementos of her childhood are preserved just as she left them when the Nazis whisked the family away. Her room was decorated just as my little girl might have done! All of the warmth of my own daughter seemed to linger around this improvised home.

But this house will be forever empty. The hollow rooms remind the world that on a cold winter day this innocent little Jewish girl was dragged down those stairs and hauled out to starve to death behind the barbed-wire world of the Auschwitz death camp.

There is no way in the world that I can ever conclude that any particle of that was God's will. Everything in Scripture says that God completely stands against the horror and bestiality of such an event.

So what shall we answer to Nick, and to Anne, and perhaps to you? I have found another explanation.

The Author of Adversity

The answer I gave Nick was that tragedy is caused by Satan. I must tell you that I have struggled to come to this insight. All my undergraduate training had given me the "absence of good" theory for evil. Yet this is not the biblical answer.

Where does tragedy originate? Satan is the source. His role in the terrible things of life had become clear to the Jewish community by the time Jesus came. And Jesus saw a major focus of His ministry to be the defeating of the one who is the author of adversity. No longer was there any mystery about evil. In fact, the New Testament doesn't talk about evil as an abstract idea. Evil was clearly a person. Our enemy is the evil one.

Initially, I struggled with this conclusion because it had not been intellectually fashionable to believe in the devil. And no one wants to appear naive, superstitious, and illiterate. But my egotism had stumbled over one of the strategies of the evil one.

Bishop Fulton J. Sheen once observed that the devil wants us to think he doesn't exist and so, "he is always circulating the news of his death."[1] Dr. Ruth Anshen put it pointedly: "This is why, unlike God, the Devil does not insist on his reality. It is, rather God who wants us to believe in the Devil and who cautions us against him so that we seek refuge with God."[2]

Today the rise of the occult has made the existence of Satan much more fashionable. On every hand we are deluged with movies like *Rosemary's Baby*, *The Mephistor Waltz*, *The Exorcist*, and other stomach-turners.

Since Satan has become a popular subject, I need to clarify what the Bible *really* says about him. The Hollywood version has given him a far better press than he deserves.

The devil is certainly never to be equated with God in power or deity. In response to the question about whether he believed in the devil, C.S. Lewis stated the biblical view of succinct terms:

> Now if by "the Devil" you mean a power opposite to God and, like God, self-existent from all eternity, the answer is certainly No. There is no uncreated being except God. God has no opposite. No being could attain a "perfect badness" opposite to the perfect goodness of God .... The proper question is whether I believe in devils. I do. That is to say, I believe in angels, and I believe that some of these, by the abuse of their free will, have

become enemies to God and, as a corollary, to us. These we may call devils. They do not differ in nature from good angels, but their nature is depraved .... Satan, the leader or dictator of devils, is the opposite, not of God, but of Michael.[3]

The problem with modern literature and cinema is that the adversity is enormously overrated as well as being over-publicized.

In another book, Lewis warned that it is unhealthy to have a great interest in these matters. We should be aware that there is a spy and saboteur in our midst, but discount him like we do the average James Bond spy exploit.[4]

The important point is to recognize Satan's role in what happens in this world. The current flurry of interest has missed biblical knowledge that Satan is the source of the tragic side of life. Much that has been blamed on God has come from the evil one. So let's get his work in perspective, also.

The Old Testament doesn't say a great deal about Satan. Basically he is a minor character. Of course, traditional Christian theology gives him the credit for the snake problem that set up the human condition in the garden of Eden (see Gen. 3). In the original Hebrew, Isaiah 14:12-14 was a song of mourning lamenting his fall because of his attempt to usurp the place of God. And, of course, we remember Satan when we think of Job's suffering. Though the theme isn't elaborated, Satan and adversity go hand in hand.

The big breakthrough in understanding the role of the evil one came during the intertestament period. What happened in the last 200 years before Christ had great significance for the ministry of Jesus.

125

Ever hear of Antiochus Epiphanes? Perhaps you haven't run across his story and the tales of the woe he caused. This first century B.C. king was the Adolph Hitler of his day. Because of his unspeakable cruelties, the Jews made the very important discovery about who sends tragedy.

Antiochus came on the scene around 180 B.C. as the ruler of Palestine. A descendent of the Greek conquests of Alexander the Great, this heartless fiend decided to impose Greek culture on all peoples. By his edict the Jews would put away the things of God and become Hellenists. Those who didn't conform were annihilated.

Were the penalties severe? Well, here's a sample! Antiochus outlawed circumcision because it offended Greek ideals. Of course, this ritual was crucial to being a Jew. So, if a mother had her child circumcised she faced an unbelievable penalty. First, the priest who circumcised the baby was killed. Second, the baby's father was killed. Then the baby was killed. Further, the putrefying body of the dead infant was tied around the mother's neck to be worn like a necklace!

Many other terrors were visited on the Jews. The peculiar twist to this persecution is that evil fell on those who were obedient to the commands of God. Terrible things happened as a result of their being loyal. The Hebrews faced a complete reversal of the principle of divine retribution. Now they suffered for being good! They were punished for doing the very things God had promised to bless. How could this be?

So they began to rethink the role of this strange figure they remembered from the old Scriptures. He had been mentioned by name only three times in the whole Old Testament canon. In Job he was a definite part of the difficulty. In Zechariah 3:1,2 the strange one was the source of false accusation against the high priest. Further, in 1 Chronicles 21:1, he had caused David and Israel considerable problems.

From these passages and their own experience, the Jews were able to get a clear picture of the warfare that was going on in the world. In surveying the conclusions the Jews drew from this period, Dr. James Kallas says:

> The one thing that the Jew is seeking to assert
> in his insistence on the fall of Satan is that
> *God is not the author of tragedy!* The vicious
> destruction of human life, the searing batter-
> ing of human detiny, is not the will of God. It
> is the work of God's enemy ... God is not
> evil. He does not cause unfair pain or undue
> suffering. It is in the enemy of God that much
> violence finds its bitter seed.[5]

This was the background to the coming of Jesus as the Messiah.

Martin Luther's dictum to describe the ministry of Jesus was that He came "to defeat the devil in all his works and all his ways." And from the very beginning the ministry of our Lord was aimed at bringing down the kingdom of evil. The prelude to Jesus' work is given in Matthew 4. Here Jesus squarely faces all the tempta-tions of the evil one and defeats him.

The very miracles of Jesus were an assault on the fortress of evil. Alan Richardson notes:

> All the miracles of Jesus are signs to those
> who have eyes to see, revealing who Jesus is.
> His power over the "demons" is a sign that
> Beelzebub's Kingdom is being cast down, that
> the "strong man" is being bound (Mark 3:22-
> 30, Matthew 12:15-27, Luke 11:17-23).[6]

In fact, Dr. Kallas argues that the proper understanding of the miracles of Jesus is that they are all an attack on Satan. In each instance Jesus defeats a particular work of the evil one.[7]

And notice what Jesus did. He healed the sick, He fed the multitude. He released men from the possession of evil. And, finally, He raised men back to life from the grip of death. In each instance this was a condition caused by Satan.

So as I went back to the Bible with these insights, I was amazed to discover that all of our conditions of need are clearly seen as the work of Satan. Jesus described an illness as the product of Satan's work (see Luke 13:16). Paul said the same thing (see 2 Cor. 12;7). Jesus attacked the calamities of nature and famine as having their origin in the evil one. In His miracle of feeding the multitudes He demonstrated His ability over Satan's power to deprive. When Jesus rebuked the storm he rebuked Satan's power to destroy (see Mark 4:35-41). In Ephesians 6:10-18, Paul saw us locked in a battle with the same force.

So, let's mark the conclusion in red letters. The disasters of the world do not have their origin in the will of God. The evil one is the author of adversity. In fact, Jesus taught us to pray with this in mind. When the Lord's prayer is more correctly translated from the Greek it reads: "Deliver us from the evil one," not "Deliver us from evil."

When I shared these insights with Nick he found a great sense of relief. He was able to bring the pieces together and restore his ability to trust God. He could really turn his problems over to Him. In perceiving the source of tragedy, we also can discover fully how Jesus Christ is the answer.

In each of Jesus' miracles, Satan was defeated. But

most importantly in the death and crucifixion of Christ, the ultimate battle was fought and won in His resurrection from the dead. Nick discovered he could participate in this incredible promise.

> Since we, God's children, are human beings— made of flesh and blood—he became flesh and blood too by being born in human form; for only as a human being could he die and in dying break the power of the devil who had the power of death. Only in that way could he deliver those who through fear of death have been living all their lives as slaves to constant dread (Heb. 2:14,15, *TLB*).

Nick found he had taken a miraculous journey from a question mark of doom to an exclamation mark of joy.

The Final Word

I know I haven't answered all the questions about evil, suffering and Satan. There are many areas I'm still trying to uncover. But I take heart in the fact that the Bible doesn't try to give us all of the answers. Very little is said about why Satan fell and why the world has become his abode. Scripture seems to indicate certain speculations are not of value, but it still gives us the basic facts we need for getting on with life.

And here's the confidence we should have. We can have complete assurance of the will of the heavenly Father. We don't have to carry hidden, lurking doubts. Indeed, God is for us.

But what about the adversary? Are we to live in constant dread of some hidden enemy? Paul's epistles indicate we should be aware of a real battle going on and we should take the enemy seriously. Indeed, there is an active agent who is constantly interested in winning the spiritual warfare raging in the world.

However, no one should live in dread or anxious apprehension. We need only to get our answers clear. At Calvary the final battle was fought and won. Our job is to be a part of the "mopping up" operation God is conducting until the conclusion of time.

You might ask, "Well, why doesn't God just completely wipe out the problem?" After all, getting rid of the enemy would seem to simplify our lives. The Bible doesn't speak to this question but I think we do have a clue in chapters 16, 17 and 18 of the Book of Revelation. Those passages tell us something about how God handles spiritual warfare.

The earlier chapters are helping the young church understand the persecution that has been brought on them by Rome. And, seemingly, there is no reprieve from this agency of the devil. Apparently God's elect are not covered by His protection.

Then, suddenly, the writer completely turns the tables. The truth is that Rome is not the mightiest power at all. God is the one who has been at work using Rome to accomplish other purposes the church has missed. Through those hard times, there has been a powerful cleansing that has opened the way for new growth. Surprise! God has actually used the enemy for His own purposes.

Dr. Kallas in a commentary on Revelation writes:

> Things are not what they seem. Enemy merges into servant, foe becomes in the profoundest sense, friend, for he is working for the accomplishment of God's purposes. What appears in one way to be diabolical, opposed to God's will, is instead beneficial, a messen-

ger of God. That appears to be the thought of Chapter 17.[8] Maybe the heavenly Father has allowed even Satan to remain as the ultimate symbol of God's ability to use even those things that are not in His plan in bringing creative results to pass. God can even recast the works of the devil. God's power is displayed in His ability to win that final skirmish.

The awesome realization of the inevitable victory of God sent Martin Luther writing his great hymn, "A Mighty Fortress Is Our God." Luther wanted the church to sing with a thundering voice the final word. God will prevail! You can make this your song:

A mighty fortress in our God,
A bulwark never failing;
Our Helper he, amid the flood
    of mortal ills prevailing
For still our ancient foe doth seek
    to work us woe;
His craft and power are great.

Yes, he is our foe! At least now we know who the enemy is. We are clear about the source of this cruel hate. But our hymn of praise gives glory to God because the enemy doesn't hold the final word:

Christ Jesus it is he;
Lord Sabaoth, his name,
From age to age the same,
    and he must win the battle.
And though this world, with devils filled,
Should threaten to undo us, we will not fear,
For God hath willed His truth

to triumph through us.

. . . .

God's truth abideth still,
His kingdom is forever.

The final word is Christ Jesus! The final fact is that
God's truth will always abide. The cross of Christ established this certainty for time and eternity.

So when life appears to grow very quiet, when God
seems to have become silent, I remember this hymn.
When there is no miracle, I begin to hum the melody:

The Prince of Darkness grim,
    We tremble not for him;
His rage we can endure, for lo,
    his doom is sure,
One little word shall fell him.

That word above all earthly powers, "Christ Jesus it
is He." This is the final word.

Some Concluding Thoughts

If tragedy comes from God then I have a dilemma.
How can I trust God for the best if I know He is really
the source of the worst? Personally, that conclusion of
responsibility affects everything I believe. Placing the
blame is a critical issue.

Jesus made the matter very clear. The heavenly Father is not the source of malice and chaos. Our primal
as well as contemporary enemy is the evil one. The devil
has from the beginning been associated with sin, suffering, and woe. Tragedy grows from his design and his
inspiration prompts the work of evil in this world.

We have been misled by thinking of the devil in medieval terms. Inadequate images make the evil one

sound like a superstitious relic of the past. Discovering twentieth century images will give us a handle to clarify the whole problem. Not God, but the evil one, is the source of our afflictions.

Understanding this truth should also give us assurance. In the life and ministry of Jesus, the evil one has been fully encountered and defeated. While being certain about responsibility, we need to be preoccupied with the enemy. Though he is the source of affliction, the evil one no longer has control over harm's effect on us. Through Jesus Christ I know the conclusion of every one of life's transactions will be redemptive.

Some Questions to Ponder

1. Have you ever used any of the three "pain pacifiers," described in this chapter, for yourself or someone else facing pain and tragedy? Was any of them a satisfying answer?
2. When problems or tragedy strikes you do you try to take comfort in the "God's will" pacifier? Read the following Scriptures and see what picture of God they portray: Deuteronomy 31:8; Psalm 37:4; Psalm 50:15; Matthew 7:7; Psalm 138:7; Isaiah 40:31.
3. How do we in the twentieth century portray Satan? How do Scriptures describe Satan? See 1 Peter 5:8. What are some of his names? See Matthew 13:19; Luke 4:13; John 12:31; 14:30; Acts 26:18; 2 Corinthians 4:4; 11:14; Ephesians 6:12; 2 Thessalonians 2:8; 1 Peter 5:8.
4. Under the section "The Final Word" I say, "At Calvary the final battle was fought and won. Our job is to be part of the 'mopping up' operation God is conducting." How do Scriptures tell us to deal with the devil? See Ephesians 4:26,27; Ephesians 6:11; James 4:7; 1 Peter 5:8.

133

Notes

1. Fulton J. Sheen, "Temptation," in *Twenty Centuries of Great Preaching*, eds. Clyde E. Fant, Jr. and William M. Pinson (Waco: Word Books, 1971), vol. 2, p. 171.
2. Ruth Nanda Anshen, *The Reality of the Devil: Evil in Man* (New York: Harper and Row, 1972), p. 128.
3. C.S. Lewis, *The Screwtape Letters (New York: The Macmillan Co., 1947), p. vii.*
4. C.S. Lewis, *Miracles* (New York: The Macmillan Co., 1947), p. 126.
5. James Kallas, *The Real Satan* (Minneapolis: Augsburg Publishing House, 1975), pp. 43,44.
6. Alan Richardson, *A Theological Word Book of the Bible* (New York: The Macmillan Co., 1960), p. 154.
7. Kallas, *The Real Satan*, p. 75.
8. James Kallas, *Revelation: God and Satan in the Apocalypse* (Minneapolis: Augsburg Publishing House, 1973), p. 103.

seven

_____A Personal Conversation with Jesus_____

"Jesus, I get afraid. Sometimes I get very confused." I was trying to sound very philosophical and abstract when the break in my voice betrayed by feelings.

"Often everything gets blurred and uncertain. But I really do believe you are the answer to life and death—" Now my fears about death were loose and my throat was choking on the words.

There was a tender tone in Jesus' voice. "And why do you expect so much of yourself? I don't expect it of you."

I didn't want to break. Tears made me feel weak and foolish. Yet I couldn't hide what was now becoming very humiliating.

He reached out and gripped my chin. There was no way to turn. We were simply one man to another caught in a difficult moment.

"Did I not weep when Lazarus died? And do you remember my tears as I entered Jerusalem and wept over the city? Oh yes, the heavenly Father also grieves over His world. So do not fear your feelings."

I couldn't respond. I just shrugged my shoulders and made some aimless gesture with my hands. Then He added a final word.

"Fear only this. That you might never be able to feel and weep at all."

The
Inevitable
HOUR

Life is filled with inevitables. The unavoidable contingencies of living may creep up but finally they happen to us all. Because ours is a fallen world, we cannot avoid the inherent pitfalls. So pain comes to both the good and the bad and none of us is ever exempt. Suffering is too valuable and its work too important for any to miss the visitation.

So, death still makes house calls. Only one door leads out of life. The miracles of yesterday will not prevent the certainties of tomorrow. In the end, Lazarus did die.

But along the way we do not have to be victims. When there is no miracle we need not feel victimized. Perhaps that suggestion has surprised you? Nevertheless, what can't be avoided can be transformed by how we receive the experience. The bitter, brackish waters of anguish can be changed into the new wine of sensitive, perceptive personhood. Remember the water into wine miracle story started the whole miraculous ministry of Jesus.

So, with no single exception, an hour of death will confront each of us. We cannot avoid standing at the graveside of someone more dear to us than our own life. Grief cannot be avoided. And along the way other inevitable moments will rack and assault our emotions. Grief is a built-in fact of life.

But we can choose how we will encounter sorrow's sobering ministry. Certainly mourning can never be greeted as a friend but, just maybe, grief doesn't have to be our enemy either. Perhaps it can be an ally. This blunt comrade can cleanse yesterday and help our memory savor the best. Finally, through grief, we are better prepared for the future.

Therefore, let's reflect on how to deal with our emotions. Should grief call can we form an alliance of accommodation? Not only is compatibility possible, it is necessary.

Distinguishing Can from Can't

There are at least two basic life situations that cause us to have feelings of loss. Some circumstances can be changed; others cannot. The difference in the two situations has tremendous implications for how we will handle grief. Both types of crises bring grief but recognizing the difference is very important.

Chapter 3 discussed the difference between the possible and the impossible. That crucial distinction needs to be a part of our thinking right now! The difference in what can and can't be changed dictates the form grief takes. There is a difference in grieving over what might be corrected and the pain we experience over what can't ever be changed. We have to distinguish between can and can't.

Want an example of an unchangeable event that brings mourning? Well, death is the first thing that comes to mind. We all cringe at that thought. These fears loom so large that many people find even discussing death to be almost impossible.

But we grieve for other problems that are not as obvious. After an amputation, the body will grieve over the loss. The nerves keep on sending impulses, expecting action. In turn, the amputee may lapse into a depression, mourning the loss. Many women who have had mastectomies struggle with overwhelming feelings akin to the emotions encountered at the side of a casket. These undercurrents of agony are so strong because we are confronted with the inescapable.

Facing the Inevitable

Coping with a continuing and permanent affliction is probably the most difficult emotional pain any of us will ever know. In such an inevitable situation, grief may linger for years. How do we face this problem?

The doctor comes through the door. His whole demeanor signals the worst. With kindness and gentle firmness he confirms that your child will never have an I.Q. of over 40. The suspicions were always there but the unavoidable confirmation has come. A mourning begins that may take five, ten, fifteen years to fully expel.

One common denominator in these irrefutable instances of pain is a burning desire to deny the obvious. While grief has already started to form, we keep insisting that the problem just isn't so. Clinging to the possibilities of a reversal will cause our necessary grief to become a vicious enemy.

And what pain there is in recognizig the truth! In our

138

anguish to hide from the truth we develop an internal battleground in which an emotional war rages through every nerve fiber of our body. Silently in our emotional recesses, grief still waits to be observed. There is cathartic work to be done. But our hopes and dreams keep battling back the realization that what we dread will be confirmed.

My wife deals with repression and denial in her work with the mentally retarded. Again and again, parents come with their hopeful ploys trying to avoid the truth about the permanent limits of their children. So, she presents a test score indicating an I.Q. of 50. And they respond that they are willing to wait for the child to go to college later than usual! Of course, they hope she will remold their "can't" into a "can." Tragically, such will not be.

Years may be required for the hidden grief to fully surface and be acknowledged. In fact, Barbara's experience with these parents indicates that usually they require a number of years before they can completely accept their situation emotionally.

Recently, a mother shared that eight years passed before she could face the total truth. One afternoon, after forcing the child through a number of frustrating exercises, Beverly realized that nothing had changed her daughter through years of special attention. They had crossed the country looking for every new hope. Beverly had staunchly maintained she would change Karen's limitations! No mountain would be left unclimbed to put new light in those dull little eyes.

But on that cold winter day she saw through the fog to the reality. There had been no miracle and she could not perform one.

Beverly curled up on the bed in a tight ball and sobbed her heart out. For the first time in all those years she

139

cried true desperate tears of grief and defeat. The battle was over. The crushed, broken emotions of mourning rose to the surface in waves of convulsive anguish.

Hope was gone. Possibility was gone. And now she felt that even God was gone. Only one word seemed to abide—gone. Gone, everything was gone.

After an hour of wallowing in a valley of seemingly complete despair she came to her decision. For eight long years she had sidestepped reality. Would her life be one long grind of agony in struggling with an impossible affliction? Or would she live with joy and purpose while accepting the unavoidable? She sat up in bed and realized the matter was purely in her hands. Now she knew that behind her resolute denial, self-pity had lurked all those long months. Her child wasn't unhappy with life. The truth was that she, Beverly, was the only one living in misery. She would bury the past and start living with a genuine smile on her face!

In those next few minutes, several realizations began to surface. Her fierce affirmations of love were a camouflage too. She was loving Karen because she might change. She had not faced the need to love the child "as is" and let her little life be happy even with limitations. Suddenly all of those frantic exercises made no sense. They weren't really for the little one. The mother had needed the false hopes they promised.

She walked over to the little mongoloid so content with her toys on the floor. Her hands cupped the little chin and she looked down into the slanted blue eyes. Now she would love Karen for Karen's sake!

As she clutched the whimsical face to her breast, she began crying again. Now the whole temper of emotion was changed. She was crying because she was glad Karen was her child and she could be of service to such an innocent bundle of love.

The world was new! The terrain was washed clean and they could start again. No more side paths for the mother's hidden fears. Beverly was going to be happy. Starting then and there she would be happy!

Today, Beverly is a most vivacious woman. Never would you guess her life has been so heavily laden with heartache. Moreover, she is a constant witness to her faith in the sustaining power of God. That winter afternoon she really found the presence and power of the Father for the first time. Previously, she was sure God could be present only if He changed her daughter's condition. Now she knows He is just as present in what "can't" be.

Guidelines for Confronting Tragedy

How shall we live with the mountains that will not move? What can we do with those unchangeable life dilemmas? The following are practical suggestions for handling your emotions when there is no miracle.

Face the inevitable. That is easy for me to write at my desk and very difficult for you to face if you are confronting tragedy. However, it's still the most basic factor in handling runaway feelings. All of us are desperate in our attempts to avoid any truth that doesn't fit our dreams and hopes.

So start trying to trust the experts. One doctor may be wrong but a consistent diagnosis from several can't be explained away. Believe that the teachers, psychologists, and social workers aren't after you with special bad news.

Don't be afraid of your emotions. Our society does a poor job of teaching us to be frank and open with our feelings. We are taught to act appropriately and to give a good appearance. Ultimately, we end up not being sure of what is going on inside of us. So we must fear that our emotions might betray us. While we are trying to keep a stiff upper lip the bottom one becomes a traitor. And so we can't depend on the masks we wear.

Often we most fear a loss of nerve. Lurking in the backwaters of our subconscious is all the residue of our childhood fears. Should these memories emerge, we might find that our stamina would disappear. So we try to ignore the inner side. The result is we become more frenzied and frantic. Our voices go higher and we walk faster as we only go around in circles!

Just stop. Dare to halt in mid-flight. Recognize the strength, not the weakness of your emotions. You have greater reserves and resources than you think. Even your shakiness has a good purpose as a warning light that says "don't kid yourself." These feelings are cleansing and reconstructing.

So, don't be afraid of your emotions. They are far more trustworthy than you may think. Be sad, mad, glad, or whatever! But don't avoid being the real you.

God permits you to be mad at Him. You may be surprised to know that God has never had trouble handling feelings of people who were offended at Him. A number of Bible all-stars like Jonah and Paul questioned God's actions (see Jonah 4:1-5; 2 Cor. 12:7-9). And God went right on caring about them. So if you're mad at God about your problems, that's really O.K.

Often we fear that our bad feelings are so blasphemous that we can't face up to their reality. Though we don't want to say the words out loud, still the hostility is there. Of course, God always knows where our feelings are, anyway.

So start saying those awful words out loud where your ears can hear what's going on in your heart and stomach: "I'm mad at God! I'm really angry at Him!"

Maybe you will have to start with a whisper. Or you

142

might need to share this very quietly with your most confidential friend. But say those words! Then try saying the words with the level of intensity of your hurting. Perhaps you need to get in a room by yourself and scream what you feel inside: "I hate God! I hate God for what has happened to me!" Let all the pressure come out of hiding.

Here's a guarantee. No lightening bolts will hit the house. No freight trains will come smashing into the living room, and no floods will sweep you out to sea. In fact, you may be surprised to find the sky has turned a little bluer and the grass a bit greener. God truly loves you where you are and He can help you most when you're honest.

Find a fellowship or a pastor to sustain you. We weren't meant to carry the burden alone. The community of faith is far more than a self-help society. Christian fellowship prepares us to be burden bearers on behalf of all who come in need. We need the support that the church offers.

Look for Christians who are not appearance-oriented. You need people who will accept you and your situation without putting another layer of expectations on top of your own. You will require people who will love you when you are sad or happy, angry or elated.

Put your grief away when the work is over. Don't end up enjoying your misery. Some people make a career out of their tragedies. They spend years milking every last ounce of emotion out of the crisis. Grieving becomes their recreational activity.

One of my dear friends is a clinical psychologist who has lived through the death of two husbands. Two excruciating tragedies have ripped Nelda's life apart. Even years later her eyes still well with tears when she recounts the cost of recovery. But she has long since dealt with her grief and gone on to rebuild her life. In fact, she became a psychologist as the result of a constructive use of her grief.

Recently Nelda confronted a widow, who was lingering in grief, with the truth about her self-pity: "You seem to be enjoying this, don't you?" The woman recoiled, aghast at such a suggestion. Nelda continued, "You'll never get your life together until you quit making this death your hobby. Isn't it time to pack those experiences away like his old clothes you sent to the Salvation Army?" Though the woman was taken aback, she came to recognize her need.

"There is an appointed time for everything . . . A time to tear down, and a time to build up . . . . A time to mourn, and a time to dance . . . . A time to tear apart, and a time to sew together" (Eccles. 3:1-7). There is a time to turn again.

Everything Can Be Faced

Hurting makes us want to retreat. Certainly the tendency to withdraw is natural and understandable. In fact, if the problem has emotionally overwhelming consequences, we may find ourselves almost turning into a recluse.

Today, many people have slid into life-styles centered around avoidance. In my book, *Your Churning Place*, I discuss my tendency to become an escapist. Chapter 4 is entitled, "Escapism—Checking Out." Disaster creates reverberations that send us running for a cave. But, of course, this isn't the answer. Perhaps, that chapter will help you deal with your inclination to retreat.

Jesus was completely aware of how grief can turn us inward. He knew that retreat was not the answer for His people. His assurance was, "Fear not, little flock; for it is your Father's good pleasure to give you the kingdom"

(Luke 12:32, *KJV*). His people are always moving through present difficulties on to kingdom-living. And kingdom-living is simply a way of talking about a contemporary life-style that already has the power God will finally use to heal all hurts at the end of time. That help will enable us to face everything that enters our lives.

Failure to grasp these answers keeps us from being of help to the present age. Often, people assume that if they deny their fears, griefs, and anxieties, their internal boiling waters will evaporate. And that just isn't so.

I remember trying to help a lady deal with the fact of her sister's alcoholism. Obviously, the issue was deeply charged and had become painful for her to face. While believing God could heal her sister's need, she was almost completely overcome with emotion. Clearly, she wanted to cry and needed to release her grief.

However, as she began to break down her husband leaped to her defense. With a fierce look of displeasure, he dramatically changed the conversation. Intently his hostile gaze warned me not to get back on the subject of the alcoholic sister. Helplessly, I listened to us drift off into pointless conversation about the weather. As they left in smiles I knew the poor woman was bleeding internally with grief over her sister. The husband couldn't face the emotion.

But everything can be faced! Not only the fears created by outside circumstances, but the inner fears of doubt and inadequacy can be completely faced and defeated as well. We have this complete assurance in Jesus Christ.

Matthew's remembrance of Jesus' last words was a total confidence in the new power God gave for everyday living: "All authority has been given to Me in heaven and on earth .... Lo, I am with you always, even to the end of the age" (Matt. 28:18,20). Since our Lord

145

said His physical good-bye in those terms, we know that His spiritual presence is with us in every need and crisis. Certainly, He is not afraid of any issue in life. And now we don't have to be fearful either.

Grief I cannot avoid. But grief I can afford. Even Jesus wept.

Some Concluding Thoughts

The Bible gives us pictures of gigantic men of towering faith. These warriors of God fought lions bare-handed, crumpled nations with swords, and even walked through fire unburned. Yet, they had moments of deep doubt, overwhelming fear, personal indecision, and were also betrayed by their own emotions. Should we feel guilty when we are no different? Certainly, Jesus never asked this.

Look everything in the eye. If God be sovereign, then nothing needs to be hidden. When tragedy is irreversible, then begin working your way through whatever must be faced. Do not hesitate to open every floodgate that must be crossed. Recognize how tentative and fragile your emotions are. Your faith is not betrayed because your emotions are made tender by fear.

Should the difference in the possible and the impossible not be clear, don't try to dictate the shape of the future. Accept the sovereign hand of God to sort out the possibilities. Remember that regardless of the turning of the tides, the heavenly Father is the source of our adequacy. The answer has never been in you, anyway.

Some Questions to Ponder

1. What emotion do you fear most? Which ones do you try to conceal?
2. This chapter suggests that it's alright to be mad at God. How do you feel about this idea? How do you

think God would handle your being angry at Him? Read about some people in Scriptures who rebuked God or were angry at Him: Numbers 11:10-15; Jonah 4:1-11; Habakkuk 1:1-3.

3. Do you have a pastor, another person or a support group with whom you can level? Are you a person that someone else can turn to for unburdening?

4. What does Jesus' promise in Matthew 28:20 mean to you personally?

eight

_____A Personal Conversation with Jesus_____

"Master, why must we wait?" I was feeling the pressure of my own needs and wanted immediate results. "Why does the heavenly Father seem to linger so long in many of the things that He does?"

Jesus reflected for a moment. Then He turned and pointed to the mountains at our back. "What do you see?"

Well, what was there to say? I had seen the hills and mountains thousands of times. "I can see trees, valleys and the rocky top of the cliffs. That is all there is."

"All there is?" Jesus smiled.

I realized I had made His point by my response.

"All there is. And do you not know that just behind that range lies the ocean? A great deal more is there!

"We see mountains and obstacles and believe that is the complete picture. But the Father sees clear through into eternity. His vision encompasses the oceans and the forests that lie out there in tomorrow.

"We wait impatiently for today's answers. But they can be found only among tomorrow's secrets. The Father alone knows these secrets. And so we wait."

149

While Waiting for a MIRACLE

Don't forget that I *do* believe in miracles! One of the assurances I have as I encounter tragedy is that God does intervene in an unexpected and powerful way. I believe Saint Augustine was exactly right. God is always working through a set of higher laws that we just don't yet understand. And in accord with His grand design for all of creation, He is constantly breaking into everyday life with His power.

These higher laws sometimes are the reason that God doesn't immediately bring to pass the result we want. At the same time, through the same principles, God does spectacular things. Miracles do happen all the time.

Never would I subtract a word of promise from the hope that God's hand still heals brokenness. Many times in a dark hour I have affirmed that we shouldn't throw in the towel until we know for sure that prayer and faith have done everything feasible. Indeed, miracles still happen. So I don't want to overlook "the possible."

I can never know all that God has in mind. No one can fathom the depths of the Father's intentions. So when His intervention is a possibility, I pray—expecting a miracle.

But, while I am faithfully waiting for God's intervention, I must be aware that a powerful emotional reaction is still working within my body and soul. Though I'm convinced something can change, I still may have very strong feelings of apprehension. Often, I don't want to face these feelings lest they subvert my faith. If they surface maybe it will be a sign to God that I don't *really* believe. Then God won't do anything! So my need is compounded by fear.

You may have total confidence that God can touch cancer and it will be cured. Perhaps you have seen the lame walk. Yet, when the diagnosis of blindness or a tumor is yours personally, a jolt runs through every fiber of your entire nervous system. You cannot avoid the effect of uncertainty.

While anticipating a miracle, face these feelings of fear, apprehension and anger with complete honesty. Don't hesitate to look yourself in the eye. God's work doesn't depend on your emotions, so, you don't have to hide them from Him. He already knows how you feel deep in your heart. Read Psalm 139. Every emotion and condition of life is named in that description of God's searching presence. He is everywhere, within and without! "Where can I go from Thy Spirit? Or where can I flee from Thy presence?" (Ps. 139:7). God understands how uncertainty affects us.

I've had faithful, devout people confide that they feel

their emotions betray them. One woman said, "Suddenly I just burst out crying. I don't know why I do such silly things because I know God is going to come through." Yet, she was sure her tears were a sign of bad faith. Such wasn't the case. Apprehension was working its way to the surface.

Those uncontrolled expressions are O.K. They are a form of grief as we struggle with painful alternatives. Certainly they don't offend God.

We must accept our humanness. Anxiety is built into our condition. So even when we have confident faith, we cannot avoid thinking about disaster. When our minds start contemplating disaster, all of our emotions follow. The only real problem is when we try to deny this is happening. Then the tension *really* mounts!

Concealed and denied tension can destroy marriages and close relationships. The more we deny our emotions the more we develop a pressure-cooker mind waiting to explode.

Hiding our anxiety may also cause us to project our feelings on others. Either with a lashing tongue or through constant eroding jabs, we thrust our unexamined feelings onto others. One moment we are talking of trusting God. In the next breath, we may accuse friends and family of the very doubts that are hidden in us. The truth is we are only struggling with our inner unresolved contradictions.

So are you trusting God for a miracle? And everything points to His intervention? Magnificent! But be honest and lucid about your feelings. Struggling with apprehension is not a mark against your faith.

Encouragement for Endurance

The guidelines in the previous chapter for confronting tragedy also encourage our endurance. But if we are seeking a miracle we need some additional help. Here are three principles for holding your ground emotionally while you wait.

Don't practice wishful thinking. Wishful thinking isn't faith. We all know about children who pray for candy and want God to turn spinach into ice cream. Little ones even experiment to see if they can persuade the powers that be. While we smile at their naivete, we might be practicing the same prayer line.

Don't predetermine what God must do and how He must do it! Be open to all possibilities. Remember, the miraculous comes in many disguises. By looking for the most dramatic, we may overlook the simple interventions that are the more profound.

Don't try to psyche yourself out. Faith shouldn't ever be confused with enthusiasm. The real measure of belief isn't emotion but trust. Our heavenly Father doesn't use a spiritual thermometer on us. A feverish faith condition isn't what merits His action. No, His movement on our behalf springs purely from objectives of His love.

We need to grow in the ability to trust Him and to lean on Him with complete assurance. That trust may or may not have anything at all to do with the level of our emotions. Your doubts and fears don't scare God off. Neither will phony pep talks prompt Him to action. Be yourself and be assured He is always Himself.

Don't make bargains with God. When I go to Mexico City, I go out to the magnificent Cathedral at Guadalupe. Even now, men and women are crawling on their knees across the streets and over rough cobblestones into the church. They are keeping some strange bargain made with God. If He will intervene they will make this painful pilgrimage. Primitive? Certainly. But don't we do the same, only on a slightly different basis and usually for higher stakes?

As our emotions are surging and ebbing, we attempt to strike a special deal with God. If He will perform, then we will promise something that we otherwise would not do. And the result? Well, sometimes we're not sure if God did or did not accept the bargain. We have vague guilt or apprehension about our promise. And worse, we have turned our heavenly Father into a cheap street vendor.

No, God is not a divine bargain hunter in search of someone's emotional garage sale. Get to know Him as your Father. Jesus reminded us that this Father is not one who gives stones for bread or snakes for fish. The nature of our heavenly Father is to provide the best for our need. (See Matt. 7:7-11.)

When You Can't Tell the Difference

But what if you are caught in that hazy middle zone between the probability of a miracle and being unable to discern that the marvelous will never happen? Sometimes we cannot distinguish between the possible and the impossible.

Can and can't are not so easily and quickly separated. So one of the most frustrating issues is knowing on which side of God's miracle-working power we stand. The blurring of the middle ground can make our own decisions seem quite fuzzy and out of focus. What do we do when the alternatives are unclear?

The first step is to try and come to a neutral ground within your own heart. Notice I said "try." Unquestionably a middle attitude is elusively difficult to find. But we must attempt to not dictate our answers and to be open to any variation God sends. Just coming to a personal neutral position is probably 90 percent of the battle for stability.

When I am in neutral I have a foot planted on each

side of the line between the possible and the impossible. While I am praying and trusting God to be able to change the vinegar in my life into nectar, I am also willing to drink the cup "as is." Even such a thought is entertained with reluctance! Yet openness is essential to balance.

My next stepping-stone is recognizing God's sufficiency. When I've settled the question about whether He is able, I gain the needed confidence. In knowing He is truly the great door opener, I can quit searching for handles all the time.

That passage in Psalm 139 says that God holds all of yesterday and everything of tomorrow in this moment before Him. He looks into my life with a vision and loving concern that connects my past to His plans for the future. Far from desperate and alone, I am linked with everything that has been and ever will be! Only God is able to calculate the worth of what now may appear worthless.

I've discovered that neutrality lends its own special insights. For example, there have been times when I staunchly insisted on a preconceived set of circumstances as having to be God's will. Therefore, I knew I could claim a miracle! Yet, later I discovered that these very certainties were wrong. In my emotional confusion I actually was insisting on the wrong path.

Let me describe one such painful venture. Barbara and I had befriended an unwed mother who was caught without money or direction. Our congregation had pioneered a program for unwed mothers, and many needy women came to be housed in the homes of the church people. When a child was born it could be placed with a Christian couple should the girl choose, or the mother could keep her infant.

A particularly emotionally distraught 25-year-old

155

woman came to our door. Because she was unusually difficult we decided to take her into our own home. After a very trying period of several weeks she had the baby and wanted to give the child to a good home. Papers were signed before a judge and the child went to a couple serving in full-time Christian work.

The "happily ever after story" was shattered two months later when the baby's mother showed up with a lawyer to sue us for the return of the child! We were aghast. No girl had ever been more difficult nor received more affection and concern than she. Yet, here she was threatening and embarrassing us and the church before the world.

I knew absolutely what God's will had to be. This trial would be over in a matter of hours. The law was completely on our side. Moreover, the adopting couple were outstanding Christian leaders. An army of people were praying with them that the baby would not be troubled. No neutrality was needed for this. God's intentions were clear.

With a crash of the gavel the roof fell in. The judge ruled against us. The opposing lawyer claimed to have found a loophole in the wording of the long-standing standard relinquishment form. The judge decreed the child would have to be returned to its biological mother. Across the city and state the papers carried the story. Social workers and adopting parents were shocked. How could such a ruling be given on such absurd grounds? Yet the verdict came and the room went silent. The future seemed to go blank.

At that moment the grief began to swell up in every-one of us. Our lawyer was so shaken he couldn't go home that afternoon. My wife and I huddled in the corridor with our social worker. We grieved not only for the decision but for the future of the child. Worse was the long distance call to tell the new parents the tragic news. Their grief would be unspeakable.

For days I anguished over this impossible turn of events. Our whole family went into an extended period of mourning. Crepe hung around every conversation. And the anguish would not depart. We knew that the appeal would take months. Ultimately, the case did go to the state supreme court.

My heart ached most for the couple. Since they were out of the state there wasn't any way the baby could be taken for the moment. They were prepared to take flight, even into Canada if necessary. Their weeks were filled with the additional uncertainty of becoming fugitives.

Why? Why? Why could this happen? One evening I confided my despair to a professional Christian worker who was a mutual friend of the adopting couple. I expressed my regrets that this family had been plunged into such a confusion. His response was immediate.

"Oh no! Don't feel that way." He seemed to have a special insight. "I was with Jim and Merna. Never in their lives have they known such an experience of grace and power. These days have tempered their faith and character as nothing else has done. These months have given them priceless maturity. No, they are grateful for this trial."

His words lingered with me late into the night. Slowly, I began to recount the numerous insights, the new encounters, and even unexpected opportunities for ministry that had grown out of these hard days. All of us now looked at our own children in a new light. We had become critically aware of how paper-thin stability is. While our grief and indignation raged, we realized a new sense of the availability of God's presence even in defeat.

157

Though we could not know, perhaps renewal had been imparted to the unwed mother. We had continued to pray for her during those months. Often we had to fight back bitter resentments, yet we prevailed in trying to be concerned for her as well.

On that night I started to see the point. All of my previously determined plans were destroyed but God's sovereign sufficiency had not been thwarted. Even before the trial began He knew the ending of the story. Never had He ceased to work. Most of all, I knew His eye remained on the small infant who mattered the most.

After a year passed, I came to my needed neutrality. Maybe the others in this drama had already arrived there. But finally I knew I could live with whatever final decree was handed down. Earlier I had planned to defy the judge and refuse to disclose the location of the baby. I was ready to go to jail before I would bend to such a decision! However, now I knew that God would be able to handle the matter without my defiant foot-stomping. My grief was spent and I rested in His answer. I was in neutral.

Another stretch of months passed and the final opinion came down from the supreme court. The lawyer called for me to come immediately to his office. Before I got off the elevator I silently prayed, "Father, into your hands I finally commit this child."

One look at his face answered every question. He was jubilant! Not only had the lower court been overturned, but the supreme court had soundly rejected the judge's opinion. We had won! The baby would stay with the parents! And, of course, our relief was mixed with concern for the girl who caused this long journey. We would never know about her.

Had there been a miracle? Had this result been God's

158

intention from the start? Or had the original decision been the product of evil's subverting God's justice? Could God have changed all the circumstances so that we wouldn't have been dealt the struggle and the grieving?

There are no answers to these questions. They are all the children of Mr. Why and just as futile. Only one conclusion lingers across these years. God in His sovereignty is always sufficient. I really can dare to be neutral. When the waiting hours do come they can drag confusion with them. But doubt, despair, and grief do not stay the hand of the Father. I have the emotional security to look within myself before I look to each day.

The apostle Peter gave us a final word of direction:

> Do you want more and more of God's kindness and peace? Then learn to know him better and better. For as you know him better, he will give you, through his great power, everything you need for living a truly good life: . . . But to obtain these gifts, you need more than faith; you must also work hard to be good, and even that is not enough. For then you must learn to know God better and discover what he wants you to do. Next, learn to put aside your own desires so that you will become patient and godly, gladly letting God have his way with you (2 Pet. 1:2,3,5,6, *TLB*).

Some Concluding Thoughts

God does intervene in our world. When He comes with power the sudden and unexpected can happen. Christians who don't know that the miracle power of God is available to them are missing a promised portion of the faith.

Yet, people with profound trust still have to wait many times throughout their lives. When God is ready to act, we have to be in step with His timetable. And His plan can be very different from ours. Certainly, waiting has its own emotional effect.

Today, many voices are telling us that God can't work unless we have the right emotional outlook. And this waiting period often creates a bad attitude. The result is that the burden of our physical problems is increased because we're afraid our negative feelings may betray our faith. Guilt can also creep in as we begin to think that maybe our apprehensions are the reason God hasn't already dramatically corrected our problem.

To the contrary, God's strength is not bound by our emotions. He is looking for our trust. And we must learn to recognize the difference between trust and feelings. God recognizes that they are different areas of life. As a child starting to move from a wall into the parents' arms, so we must trust while possibly harboring fear and concern.

Even when we are apprehensive, the strong arms of God still wait for us. Recognizing He is there, even when we feel shaky, will carry us through the hours while we wait to see what form His intervention will take.

Some Questions to Ponder

1. In this chapter I make the statement, "God's work doesn't depend on your emotions." Do you agree with this? Read Psalm 139.

2. When you want a specific answer to your prayer are you tempted to tell God when and how it must be done? Can you learn to say with David, "I trust in Thee, O Lord, I say, 'Thou art my God.' My times are in Thy hand" (Ps. 31:14,15)?

3. What do I mean when I say "Don't try to psyche yourself out?" Do you sometimes act like you are preparing for a big play-off against tragedy? Do you pep yourself up, get yourself all "faith-psyched" so that God will see your enthusiasm and give you the victory? What was the condition on which God answered the psalmist's prayer in Psalm 91:14,15?

4. Think back to a time when you made a bargain with God. If God answered your prayer do you think He did so because of the terms you set up? (Read 1 John 5:14.) Did you keep your end of the bargain?

5. Under the section "When You Can't Tell the Difference" I explain how I remain "neutral" while waiting for a miracle. Read this section again and write out some ways you can be neutral when you are waiting for God's answer.

nine

A Personal Conversation with Jesus

Even after awaking, I was still trembling. The vividness of the dream had completely undone me. As I turned back the blankets, I instinctively began to call for Him.

"Jesus! Jesus! Wake up! I must talk to you!" My voice still cracked a bit.

He raised to look at me from across the embers of the dying fire. Concern and caring were in His eyes.

"Master, I'm sorry to wake you, but I was frightened. I dreamed of my death. My death, it was my death! " I did not want to sound hysterical but panic oozed out.

Jesus was calm and steady. He responded with a reassuring tone, "What did you see?"

"I saw myself walking across the deck of a great boat. In the frozen night the vessel seemed bound for a distant port. Wind blasted across the deck. As I came to the rail, I realized I was peering into a vast emptiness. There was no bottom or ceiling to the night, only eternal emptiness. I was terrified!"

He leaned forward. The glow of the campfire came up from the ashes to cast shadows across His face. Then He spoke very deliberately.

"Indeed, one day you will look death in the eye. Yes, the time will come when you will peer into the void again. But do not let your dreams trouble you." He paused, and His voice became intense. "For when you cross the last bridge and look into eternity, the night will not be empty. My face will greet you there."

When I
Lay Me Down
to
SLEEP

"And of course, death is the greatest miracle of all."

Her assertion stopped me in mid-conversation. The twist of her words made my mind take a new turn. I liked that phrase. Her quiet confidence was absolutely correct.

Sharon was relating the final hours of Joe's life. During the long, lingering illness she had ample time to reflect on each unfolding step.

"Yes, death is the final healing, Robert."

Certainly Sharon had prayed again and again for a miracle of health. Her unceasing petitions for wholeness ascended daily. Yet the final hours came and passed in the night.

"But now I know Joe is complete. For the Christian, death is really not a defeat but a miracle." Sharon's voice became quiet and intense. "Though we looked for another intervention, we found God's greatest miracle."

What a surprise! When death seemed inevitable, the first chapter began with the plea for "something more." Now in the end we hear that death is itself a "something more." Hopefully, in between, our emotions have clarified and our vision expanded.

The ultimate objective of the heavenly Father's strategy is to bring us to a place of complete confidence. When we walk by such faith we can tolerate the absence of the usual road maps and street lights. The darkness has lost hold. We have an inner light that will not fail. Immature faith carries on endless discussions concerning the need to trust God for miracles. But maturity walks on into darkness with a strong confidence in God when there is no visible miracle.

So, in the name of a ripened faith, I want to share a personal closing word about God's intervention and the final enemy, death. Quite possibly a hidden, unfaced fear lurks behind our demand for a miracle. Our urgency arises from fear of having to confront our own dying. Many have given confident testimonies of possessing eternal life while they live in sheer terror of their own personal moment of transition. For them, the quest for a miracle is an attempt to escape from the inevitable moment.

What a hard subject. We just don't like to talk about death. Our whole society avoids the subject. Our funerals are developed and conducted to give the careful appearance of "how natural we look." Once sex was taboo and death was a common topic. Now sex is commonly discussed and death is the unmentionable subject.

Not so for Christians! The bomb has been defused and a candle lit in the darkness. Death should settle into a comfortable resting place that completes the spectrum of life's experiences. Rather than avoiding it or living in retreat, Christians can, with assurance, look forward to the ultimate stepping-stone experiences. And the source of such confidence?

Christ and Cross

My hope lies in two basics: Christ and Cross. In the cross lies the victory over death and through Christ comes my answer for life. Hope is anchored here.

The apostle John struck fire with these signs and their meaning:

> And the witness is this, that God has given us eternal life, and this life is in His Son. He who has the Son has the life; he who does not have the Son of God does not have the life. These things I have written to you who believe in the name of the Son of God, in order that you may know that you have eternal life (1 John 5:11-13).

Living with uncertainty about your death and eternal situation is totally unnecessary! If by faith you have Jesus Christ living in your life then you should have complete confidence. You know the future doesn't hinge on your performance. Christ and Cross make every tomorrow a gift. So, John wanted every person who trusts in Jesus Christ to live with absolute knowledge about today, tomorrow and forever.

The man of the world's reaction to death ranges from being apprehensive to being afraid. At best, dying is stepping over a threshold into an unknown that might be tolerable. At worst we may totally cease to exist.

Often collegiates kick nonexistence around as an interesting philosophical football. But once they face and feel obliteration, a wave of terror and meaninglessness crashes through body and soul. Their lives dissolve backward into absurdity.

What a contrast! To those who know that the face of God is revealed in Jesus of Nazareth, death is the final miracle. Mortality is the strange knife that peels away the husk and fibers which have inhibited our ability to experience the total fullness of real living. In the space of a heartbeat our years of tedious self-improvement are completed. While it has taken endless hours of worry to come even close to our personal goals of perfection, in that solitary moment the mission is accomplished.

So when I face death I will confidently take hold of the cross. Perhaps only then, can I fully grasp the meaning of, "It is finished." Therein is a miracle. The finale is actually a prelude to the mighty chorus proclaiming, "Now life has just begun!"

Do I detect a slight reservation? Maybe you're wondering, "This is the stuff of enthusiastic sermons, but is it really the substance of life?" While sympathetic with my ideas you may have hidden questions. Do you find yourself considering, "Will those promises really hold up when I have to look death in the eye?"

You're right! There can be a difference between words and deeds! Anyone can talk abstractly about dying. But does it ring true at the point of hand-to-hand combat?

The Crisis Clarifies

So, what's my experience? Twice in my life I have come to the brink. Both times I faced the realization that my death was imminent. The first confrontation was as swift as it was nearly final. Though the second visit crept in, the awareness was far more agonizing. Let me share how the crisis does clarify.

The first time? Considering myself to be an indomitable force, I tried something very silly. During a flood I tried to swim underneath what was normally a small and refreshing waterfall. Hidden back in the rocks was an inviting little grotto. But now the waterfall had turned into a raging Niagara. So, the swim seemed manifoldly more challenging.

I didn't know the calm cave had now turned into a whirlpool. The crashing swirl of water couldn't be seen through the blinding spray that was cascading from above. As I swam near the edge, I realized the maelstrom was terribly dangerous. But in the same moment the undertow locked an icy grip around my ankles. No matter how I thrashed, I was being unavoidably sucked under the falls and into the whirlpool. Sheer terror raced through my mind.

With a last desperate gasp of air I went down into a sea of dirty brown and green water. Almost drained of breath, I was thrust up into the center of the cave. Violently I was being flung around and around in the center of a giant whirlpool. My body was being pounded by the crushing weight of water, yet I could catch little gasps of air. Like water jetting around a drain I was trapped in the vortex of the swirl.

My dilemma was clear. Slowly but surely I would be pulled further back into the undertow and trapped under the waterfall. As my energy waned and the force overpowered me I would drown.

In those seconds the chilling fingers of death reached into the center of my every dream and hope. The slow, unavoidable crunch of death would wring me out and hours later my lifeless form would bob up in the backwash of the river. Any previous speculation about dying became as childish babble up against that moment of truth.

I knew nothing of the promise of Christ and Cross for victory over death. Sheer, unadulterated horror locked my imagination. Waves of realization shot through my mind like freight trains running wild in the night. "Would drowning be painful? What would this do to my family and friends? How do you die?" But one question was the worst.

"Would I just be no more? Would I just cease to be, like a balloon that pops?" Eternal punishment didn't sound nearly as bad as just not ever "being" again. There was a total dread at the realization that I might just go out like a used light bulb.

Though each impression came in a split second, the impact seemed to carry eternity. Each effect lingered as if through my whole life I had been secretly worrying over these alternatives: "Would I just be no more?"

Each insight was followed by frantic, instantaneous prayers of desperation. I promised God any and everything imaginable. I would do anything! Go anywhere, under whatever circumstances He should choose! God had my total attention.

And an amazing thing did happen. Something began to say, "Don't panic, keep calm, stop and think." So, I began to search for a window in the sea of water and a rock wall took shape on one side. As I was whirling around I realized it might be possible to reach backwards and grab some projection or crack in the ledge. Perhaps, if I could get anchored against the wall, I might drag myself out of the current.

And I did! With my body being pummeled on the surface of the water like bait in a roaring river, I pulled myself free of the deadly drain. At the cave's edge, I leaped forward like an olympic swimmer who skims the surface at a furious pace.

Exhausted, I dragged myself up on the grass. My

169

fatigue was nothing compared to the spiritual desperation that rattled around in my head. Never again could
death be a joke or merely a philosophical discussion.

Several years later the words of 1 John 5:11-13 were
unfolded to me: "And the witness is this, that God has
given us eternal life, and this life is in His Son. He who
has the Son has the life; he who does not have the Son
of God does not have the life. These things I have written to you who believe in the name of the Son of God,
in order that you may know that you have eternal life."

How well I knew of the depths that these verses
plumbed! That watery grave that almost claimed my life
was still vivid in my mind. The next time I came to the
final abyss, I wanted to know that everything was under-
written. So, I prayed and asked the Holy Spirit to give
me His assurance about eternal life.

In the days following that prayer, I began to have a
growing inner awareness that my name really was firmly
etched into the Bible's promise: "And the witness is this,
that God has given Robert Wise eternal life ... "
Though the crushing sound of the cascades stayed with
me as a lingering phobia, I knew I could face the ultimate rush of mighty waters.

The Profit in the Promise

Promise and problem were tucked away for other
days. One by one the years of adulthood unfolded. Once
again death slipped back into the mental files of
probabilities to be considered upon reaching the age of
65. The vitalities of a full life left no time for morbid
speculations.

And then the phone call came in the middle of the
afternoon. I had been sick with some form of virus for
several weeks. But forgetting my vulnerability I had
kept right on working! Two days before, I had preached

a sermon with a temperature of 103 degrees. (My, what noble faith!) Finally I had gone to see the doctor but immediately returned to the firing line at the office. He ordered me to go home to bed but the press of the ministry seemed more urgent. And then the test results came back and his phone call followed.

I had nephritis!

No, there is no medication or treatment. Yes, it is very serious. Why? Because I would lose my kidneys. They would start to shrink and in the end must be removed unless something reverses the course of the disease.

The doctor's warning was solemn. I had ignored the signs of illness and the result was a secondary infection that couldn't be treated. Rest seemed to be the only hope. All we could do was watch and see. And pray.

I became progressively worse. Finally, I was sleeping 15 to 20 hours a day. I would awake for a few moments and then drop back into deep sleep. When I was alert my whole body ached and my joints were sore and irritated.

My wife began her own investigation into this strange illness. The medical encyclopedias stunned her. The data left the same impact on me. Once again I was going under the waterfall. This time the whirlpool would not be satisfied by any dramatic burst of athletic energy. The matter was completely and totally out of my hands.

On one of those fall afternoons I awoke after sleeping one whole night and one whole day. Strange dreams and visions had been tiptoeing through my slumber. Their sum total meant that my unconscious mind was fully aware of being in the vortex of a whirlpool. The sinking realization of mortality was again rising in the pit of my stomach.

A new specter moved into my bedroom. The haunting awareness that life would march on quite well without me perched at the foot of the bed. As I stared into this waking dream I could see how the family would have to make adjustments but they would go on. As hard as it might be, the children would grow up and, perhaps, my wife would remarry. With all of the grief and longings of love, they would remember but go on without me.

Whenever and wherever you come to your own particular moments of awareness of finality, you will feel a cloak of loneliness settle in like an overwhelming, impenetrable fog. Recognition may send you on a denial trip of such magnitude you will do anything to erase the experience from memory. You may vow never to venture into that door again. Should you take that route you soon will find yourself battling almost irresistible depression. Though you resist pinpointing the source, you cannot avoid the effect.

But that afternoon a new dimension opened before me. As I dared to look the grim visitor in the face, I saw dawn's light! At first there was a tiny flicker of brightness and then the rays of insight began to fall over every doubt. In the end, the fog of gloom evaporated. No, this time I wasn't in a whirlpool. On second examination, I was held in the palm of the Father's hand.

As doubt seemed certain, the ancient phrase became determined: "He who has the Son has life." As I went from one doubt to the next, the phrase always surfaced with the final word, "He who has the Son has life." Even as I rounded all the bases and came sliding in for the home plate of self-pity, I heard the promise again, "He who has the Son has life."

Could that promise hold when I was in dialogue with death? Emphatically, yes!

That afternoon I knew death had lost its sting. I watched the leaves falling from the trees in the backyard. There was an autumn feeling surrounding my life.

Confidence reigned supreme. Whatever winter winds should follow could be met by Christ and Cross. To have the Son is to have life right now!

Amazingly enough in 24 hours after these realizations, my fever dropped and I began making a quick recovery. The next medical tests revealed my kidneys had begun functioning normally. I have no doubt that, miraculously, God touched my body.

But, even more, I am thankful for the way in which my fears and doubts were healed. During those fall days I found the absolute confirmation that the Everlasting Arms are underneath and that they do hold. Today, I know that at the final point of shedding this mode of living, I will go right on having life in Christ.

To my knowledge every member of my family lives with this same awareness. They have invited Jesus Christ to be a part of their lives. The Scripture assures me that no man or power can remove any one of them from the Father's hand. So I have absolute confidence for them as well.

There are six of us: a mother and father, three boys and one girl. Some day we will stand beside the bed of one of us in a last critical hour. We have already come close several times. And, of course, when the time arrives we will all be praying for a divine intervention. But should there be no miracle, we can know that for us death has its own wondrous dimension. He or she who has the Son will already go on having life.

The promise holds.

What Shall We Behold?

One further clue is hidden in John's little discourse. "To have the Son" has another ramification. In death we will come fully face to face with our Christ.

Christian people commonly talk about death as "going to be with Jesus." Sometimes this comes across in such sentimental terms that the phrase sounds syrupy and phony. Tasteless funeral music reduces the power of the phrase to culturally void clabber. Nevertheless, the figure of speech has overwhelming promise.

The miraculous converting power of death opens our eyes to see what before could only be believed. Our ears are opened to hear what otherwise was only felt. Our hearts express what previously was solely a dream. Indeed, we will be face to face with the risen Christ!

But I already have an inkling of what He will look like. For at least 20 years a story has bounced around in my memory. From the plot I developed my expectations of what is just over the invisible line.

As a teenager I heard Cecil Henson tell his "death story" many times. He was one of those brilliant, sensitive people that happens occasionally to a small town.

Incredibly, in 1940 Cecil was pronounced medically dead for approximately 20 to 30 minutes. During those lost minutes he entered one of those extraordinary adventures of leaving his body and this world behind. During this period of being dead he discovered a number of things that defy the imagination. Ultimately he felt God directing him to return to this life and to rear his small son, Van.

He came back to dedicate his life to raising the boy who would otherwise have been orphaned. Van's mother had died in childbirth and Cecil had not gotten over the blow. During those missing minutes his hostilities disappeared and he was ready to pour himself into the little lad. Ultimately, Van grew to be an outstanding person. Today he is an oral surgeon and countless lives have been touched by his faith as well as his medical skill.

And what happened to change Cecil's life so dramatically? During that period of "twilight" he encountered Jesus in person. In those moments he looked fully into the face of the risen Christ and beheld Him in all of His glory.

It is Cecil's description of His face that has gripped my imagination through the years. He saw the face of Jesus as a marvelous mosaic made up of a hundred small facets. Each piece added a shade or line to the total picture. So in looking into this composite face he could see the countenance of Christ. But as he looked, he could see a hundred parts.

The startling realization was that the mosaic pieces were not tile, metal, or glass. Each small section was a clear, distinct cameo of someone's face. As Cecil stared fixedly at the face there was a pulsating fluctuation between the total face and the cameo sections. One minute he could see the Face and then, in the next he was aware of hundreds of faces.

In awe Cecil began to recognize what was revealed in each of those cameos. They were all people he knew! Moreover, they were all people who had loved him and given him kindness during his life. He could see an aunt and an uncle. And there was his mother and on the other side his father's face moved into focus. School teachers, friends, associates, people who had already died before him. And now through their graciousness and goodness they had become a part of conveying the human picture of Christ.

Overwhelmed in worship and amazement, Cecil bowed before the risen Lord. In the lingering moments of that experience, anxieties, fears and doubts were healed. When Cecil "returned" to start his life again, the face of Jesus guided him through the years ahead. Christ and Cross remained sufficient for him until, over 20 years later, he died.

When the Seasons Turn Again

Another day I will come to the final autumn of my life. I fully expect some of the same reservations and misgivings to call again. And as on that other autumn I will have to speak to them in the name of Christ. I suspect this time it will be much easier than the last.

But when the time has come to lie down and not raise up again, I will not be troubled by the question of miracles. Either way the future goes will be a miracle for me. And should it be the time of transformation, I hope to skip over the line with a light jump. There will burn in me the anxious desire to find and look into the face of my Christ. I fully expect that in seeing Him I will in the same moment see all those whom I have loved. Everything will be complete, because I already have the Son in my life. In that complete moment, with the Son, I will have everything else.

And with such conviction and confidence I will lay me down to sleep.